# WHAT A
# MISTAKE!

# WHAT A

## MISTAKE!

Illustrated by *LARRY*

Written by *DAVID HARDY*

First published in Great Britain

in 1983 by

Octopus Books Limited
59 Grosvenor Street
London W1

Text and illustrations © 1983 Hennerwood
Publications Limited

ISBN 0 86273 090 2

Made and Printed in Great Britain by
Richard Clay (The Chaucer Press) Limited
Bungay, Suffolk

# CONTENTS

# Transports Of Delight

*................. Errors concerning travel and transport ....*

# Home, James

Prince Andrew, fresh (if that is the word) from his holiday with the talented actress Koo Stark, was being driven home across London after an evening in similarly sociable company. The chauffeur swung the limo down the Mall and into the Royal Mews. He then garaged the car and locked up before strolling away in the direction of home, a mug of cocoa and bed.

He was well on his way before he realized that he had left the Prince in the car! The highly-embarrassed chauffeur raced back to the garage to find the Royal personage still sitting in the back, quietly awaiting release.

'I would be frightfully grateful if you could deliver me to the right address in future' was H.R.H.'s only comment.

# The Sinking Sun

Japan's first nuclear-powered ship, the *Mutsu*, was launched proudly in 1969.

However, it failed to leave port.

Local fishermen, fearful that a nuclear accident might endanger the scallops on which their livelihood depended, picketed the harbour entrance.

The great ship spent the next four years in port.

In August 1974 the *Mutsu* made a bolt for it under cover of darkness. Only yards beyond the harbour wall, the ship developed a radiation leak. The enraged fishermen blockaded the bay and refused to allow the floating albatross to return to dock for repairs.

Similar lack of enthusiasm being displayed elsewhere, the ill-fated *Mutsu* hung around off-shore for forty-five days, until the scallop-fishermen finally relented.

Whereupon – after four years' rest – the ship limped southward to Sasebo for repairs.

Four years, £33 million later, the Japanese government announced an allocation of £120 million for the construction of a specialized servicing centre for the *Mutsu*. It will take – predictably perhaps – four years to build; during which time the floating nuclear showpiece will remain tied up in port like an overgrown bath toy.

# We'll Take Less Care Of You

For an airline that was awarded the 1982 Airline of the Year title and that blazons its caring nature across every television screen in the land, it was perhaps surprising that the British Airways PR boys did not take more care about the announcement of a new 'keep it clean' policy with regard to their passengers.

As it was, BA's medical chief, Dr Donald Mackenzie, was heard to declare that 'the feelings of the *normal* travelling public must be the airline's top priority' and that in future no special care facilities would be provided for invalids, women more than 35 weeks pregnant or those with skin complaints that might look 'repulsive to others'. Such unfortunate expressions could cost the troubled finances of BA a pretty penny, if every unfortunate acne-sufferer were to think twice before 'flying the flag'.

# Keeping An Eye Out For Lost Property

Users of public transport fairly often make that mundane yet most annoying of mistakes – leaving behind their parcels, handbags, umbrellas, etc. Many of these items find their way eventually to the relevant lost property office. Nothing very remarkable in this, you may say. But consider for a moment the forgotten articles of those who travelled on the London Midland & Scottish Railway in 1947...

These hapless creatures must have suffered not only inconvenience but also some considerable discomfort as a result of their absent-mindedness. For catalogued in the annual lost property report for that year of this august body, in addition to the usual 5,630 or so brollies, were a barrel organ, several sets of false teeth, a cage containing a calf with two heads, a three-legged cock, three artificial limbs and a glass eye!

★ ★ ★ ★

*.............Lord Stokes, then chairman of British Leyland, carved a place in the history of optimism in 1974 when he told the nation: 'The company is not lost. We are merely in a cyclical decline.'.........................*

# Howe's That!

Many citizens of Great Britain probably think that they have lost the shirts off their backs to our Chancellor of the Exchequer, Sir Geoffrey Howe.

So no doubt they were not unduly distressed to learn that Sir Geoffrey had gone one better by losing his dinner suit trousers on the Manchester sleeper train.

They were, in fact, stolen from his compartment, and reappeared some days later by the side of the tracks somewhere in Warwickshire. Missing, however, was the wad of notes – £100 in all – which the Chancellor had left in them. Symbolic, perhaps, of what happens to the 'Pound in Your Pocket'!

# Sky Highway

Motorists on the four-lane highway at Joliet, Illinois, were surprised, and even alarmed, to see a parachutist land in the middle of the road.

The 26-year-old skydiver was seized by the ever-vigilant highway patrol, who gave the matter due consideration and then, with some originality, decided on the charge: not using an authorized entrance!

# All Of A Quiver

Baggage handlers at Calgary Airport in Canada became alarmed when they heard a strange humming noise coming from a suitcase which was being transferred from one plane to another.

The local police bomb squad was summoned as a matter of some urgency. The baggage area was cleared and the bomb-hunters pumped the suitcase with air.

When this exercise did not produce even a puff of smoke, never mind an explosion, the police were emboldened to open the case.

They discovered a personal, and rather noisy, vibrator which had succeeded in turning itself on in the course of a flight from Vancouver.

# Back-Up-Front

Passengers attempting to travel on the much-vaunted British Airways shuttle between Scotland and England were convinced they were living in a wrong-headed, back-to-front world....

They were told, on checking in, that the back-up flight would leave *before* the regular flight which it was supposed to be backing up.

If you see what I mean.

★　　★　　★　　★

*. . . . . . . . . . . . . . US businessman Chauncey Depew warned his nephew not to invest $5,000 in an unknown young man named Henry Ford. He told him: 'Nothing has come along that can beat the horse and buggy.'. . . . . . . . . . . . . . . . . . . . . .*

★　　★　　★　　★

# Nicholas The First

Nicholas Cugnot was a man of great importance in the history of motoring and the motorist. A French artillery officer, he became the world's first motorist in 1769 when he invented and then drove a three-wheeled car powered by steam.

Within minutes he had notched up another first. He drove into a wall and became the first crash victim. He was not really hurt, apart from his feelings, and went back to work with a will. Soon he had improved the steering and, more important, the brakes, and was back on the road with an advanced model capable of whizzing along at two miles an hour.

Things were really looking up for Nicholas when he was contracted by the French Ministry of War to design and build a military carrier. However, it is a long road that has no turning, and Nicholas' problem was that he kept turning into trouble. After a string of crashes during road tests, he achieved his hat-trick of firsts.

He was the first motorist to be jailed for dangerous driving.

# The Longest Day

Travelling hopefully but never seeming to arrive anywhere on schedule, Mr and Mrs Thomas Elham made a no-passport day trip to Boulogne, and wound up seeing a great deal of Europe.

Having finished their shopping, the couple set out for a stroll to see the sights of the town. Unfortunately, their grasp of the French language was insufficient to enable them to understand the street signs, and they became hopelessly lost. The French people they met were very kind and eventually they got a lift to the railway station.

As the last ferry had left, the Elhams decided to go to Paris and make their way back to Dover from there. Unfortunately, they caught the wrong train and found themselves the next morning – in Luxembourg! The local police put the confused travellers on a train for Paris and they slept most of the way – all too soundly in fact, for they missed their connection and woke up in Basel!

The obliging Swiss police gave the couple directions back to Boulogne but somehow the doomed travellers lost their way again, and ended up hitchhiking over sixty kilometres to Vesoul in central France. A long-distance lorry-driver gave the bemused couple a lift to Paris, but when they reached the Gare du Nord, their troubles were not over.

'We misread the signs,' Mrs Elham explained, 'and took the train to Bonn.'

From Germany the Elhams were conveyed post haste back to France. At the border, a sympathetic *gendarme* decided to make sure the Continent was freed of this dreadful new scourge and drove the couple all the way to Boulogne.

It took twenty-four hours to persuade the Customs that their unlikely tale of misadventure could possibly be true. But at last they were allowed on to a ferry and soon the familiar white cliffs of Dover welcomed the Elhams back to their native land – and a twenty-three mile stroll back to their own front door.

# Leading By Example

Delegates attending the 1982 Confederation of British Industry Conference at Eastbourne would have aided their case against the creeping evil of increased car imports by not themselves advertising the appealing nature of the rival foreign product.

On the very day that Ray Horrocks, chief executive of beleaguered BL Cars, led the onslaught on the alien invader, hawk-eyed press men gleefully counted 17 assorted Mercedes, Citroens, Alfa Romeos and BMWs parked in the courtyard of the popular Grand Hotel awaiting the arrival of their owners, exhausted by many hours' patriotic cheering at the conference centre.

Xenophobia begins at home, gentlemen.

# Why The Lagonda Was Lagging

Woburn Abbey, ancestral home of the Duke of Bedford, has been the scene of some eccentric publicity stunts in its time. Few, however, have turned out as disastrously as that scheduled for the occasion of the 17th wedding anniversary of the Duke's son, the Marquess of Tavistock.

The Marchioness had decided to present her husband with a little 'keepsake' – a £32,000 Aston Martin Lagonda. The car had taken the 1976 Motor Show by storm, so when the story was leaked to the press, reporters and television cameras galore were on hand to witness the ceremony. The Lagonda made its appearance right on time. However, instead of the anticipated roar of exhaust and crunch of flying gravel, there arrived a stately procession of red-faced Aston Martin men pushing the mighty machine up the long drive.

Apparently, the mini-computer specially developed to revolutionize the car's controls system had blown up.

'Someone misconnected a black wire to a red one,' explained shamefaced director, Peter Sprague.

# Clocking In

Customs man Colin Fisher was approached at Heathrow Airport by an elderly American who had just flown in from Miami.

'Can you direct me to the airport Post Office?' enquired the Transatlantic voyager. 'My son is meeting me under the clock.'

Fisher was puzzled. There was a Post Office in the Terminal Three building, but certainly no clock under which people could meet in the time-honoured fashion.

Could the traveller have got it right? he wondered.

'Why certainly,' responded the American. 'Here, look, I'll show you the letter from my son.'

Sure enough, there was the instruction from the attentive offspring. The only problem was that the lad was expecting to meet his father thousands of miles away at Kennedy Airport, New York.

Somehow, the old gent had managed to get on a flight from Miami to London, instead of New York, and had also failed to notice either that he was crossing the Atlantic, or that the flight had lasted almost twice as long as the usual trip to New York.

'I guess I fell asleep and lost track of things,' he mused.

# Common Cents

The New York City Transit Authority overlooked one thing when they approved the design for the new 75c ticket machines on the subway: the slot provided would accommodate with equal success the 17½c tokens used by commuters on the road toll machines in nearby Connecticut. A fairly expensive mistake for the near-bankrupt city at over 50c net loss per journey.

Following an embarrassing exposé in the papers, New York's flamboyant Mayor, Ed Koch, decided to intervene personally to pour oil on troubled underground water.

Unfortunately, his hastily called press conference was less than a roaring success. For in announcing an all-out police initiative to stop the 'outright thieving' of the fare cheats, the grandiloquent Mayor got carried away and described the naughty commuters as 'leprous'. Only to find himself at the centre of another row, this time caused by complainants from many national lepers' charities.

# Whitehall Farce

This is quite clearly the age of the strain, if you happen to be a commuter.

Take the experience of Mr Bernard Whitehall. He was sitting on a train which he believed to be the 7.23 from Reading to Waterloo. It was not. He was actually sitting on the 7.09 from Reading to Guildford, which trundles via Ascot.

Mr Whitehall is a resourceful chap. Having discovered his mistake, he remained undaunted. When the train pulled in at Ascot, he jumped out and had it diverted to Waterloo. Just like that.

This was, of course, something of a surprise to the Guildford passengers, all of whom were obliged to put away their crosswords, get out and wait another 30 minutes for the next train to their destination.

A British Rail spokesperson commented: 'Very few people travel from Ascot to Guildford. It seemed to Mr Whitehall far more sensible that the train should be diverted to pick up the path of the 7.23, which had been cancelled.'

Perhaps I should add that Mr Whitehall is manager of BR Southern Region's south-west division.

# Time Slips By

Passengers arriving at Weybridge Station in Surrey were baffled by an announcement scrawled in inimitable BR script on an official blackboard. It appeared to announce that:

> STATION CLOCKS ARE FIVE MINUTES
> FAST DUE TO A LANDSLIP BETWEEN
> FARNHAM AND ALTON

Apparently a stray raindrop, coat sleeve or vandal's finger had deleted the requisite full stop (work it out!) and obscured the remainder of the message concerning delays to that morning's trains, rendering the notice thus more worthy of H.G. Wells than BR Tales.

# Defeated Victor

Victor Grant was a man with a simple goal in life. He wanted to buy a car and, to that end, he saved up for the happy day, a pound here and a fiver there.

Being a man who liked to give others a pleasant surprise, he did not tell his wife of his plan and kept the money he accumulated hidden in a bundle of old clothes. He had collected £500 when the dustmen called at his home in Wrexham, North Wales.

Mr Grant's wife, seeking to clear out unwanted old rubbish, unwittingly gave them the bundle.

Mr Grant was not best pleased with this news when he returned home from work. He hired a mechanical digger to plough through the local rubbish tip, but after two days' fruitless search he gave up.

He went home and started to save up all over again. But this time he put the money in a bank.

# Change For The Worse At Crewe

Sir Peter Parker, chairman of British Rail, is no stranger to the experience of getting on the wrong train.

In July 1978 he was on his way from Crewe to Carlisle for an important meeting. He arrived at the station with seconds to spare before the train was due to leave.

Flashing his BR train pass, a harassed Sir Peter dashed on to the platform and jumped aboard. But instead of snuggling into his comfortable seat on the fast train to Carlisle, the Chairman found himself speeding in quite the opposite direction, first stop Euston.

He talked a highly dubious guard into throwing a note on to the platform at Tamworth, asking those concerned to 'phone Cumbria County Council and tell them he would not be able to attend their meeting, owing to circumstances which were now completely beyond his control.

When he got to London he decided to fly back to the north, sensible fellow that he is.

# Press Gang

**Errors concerning newspapers and media** ...............

# Up The Wall Chart

*Doctor* is a weekly newspaper for general practitioners. As part of its excellent service to its readers, it produces a weekly vaccination chart which is inserted in the publication. The chart shows, on brightly coloured maps of the world, what jabs are required and where.

Doctors, and indeed *Doctor*, know a great deal about anatomy. Unhappily this knowledge does not stretch to geography or even the recent history of the African continent. The map still in use in 1982 had a distinctly imperial echo. It clearly showed Southern Rhodesia where Zimbabwe is (and plain old Rhodesia was before it). Even odder, half the map of the dark continent was given in French.

Perhaps, if there is a doctor in the house, a new atlas could be prescribed for *Doctor*.

★　　★　　★　　★

. . . . . . . . . . . . . .*A travel article in* Ulster Magazine *reported:* '*The nearest hotel was five miles away in one direction and practically 12 in the opposite direction.*'. . . . . . . . . . . . . . . . . .

★　　★　　★　　★

# Paper Chase

An irate woman reader telephoned the offices of the *Washington Star* to complain that her edition had not been delivered for a couple of days. She was told that this was hardly surprising, seeing that the *Star* had gone out of business more than a year before and only a few accountants were left in the place tidying up the few loose financial ends that remained. They suggested to the reader that she might be thinking of the illustrious rival newspaper, the *Washington Post*.

The woman was most indignant. 'Certainly not,' she insisted. 'I never read the *Post*. It's definitely the *Star*.'

With such loyalty, how did the paper ever go broke?

# Bottom Of The Form

*The Sun* got little that was more revealing than a cold shoulder when it tried to enlist girl students as Page Three lovelies. The super soaraway scheme was called The Nudie-Varsity Challenge and executives of the paper (known to its staff as *The Beano*) sat back and waited for sexy snaps of 'blue-stocking beauties' to cascade on to their desks.

They were doomed to disappointment. The student magazine at Cambridge University stiffly refused to publicize the event. A student spokesman at Manchester University told *The Sun*: 'You'll get a violent reaction if you try it here.' The National Union of Students was similarly unhelpful. It sniffed: 'Page Three is grossly sexist, insulting to women and debasing.'

*The Sun* attacked them all for being stuck-up, but in the end the whole idea turned out to be just a boob.

# Foggy Period

An issue of *Arab News* regretted:

*We are unable to announce the weather. We depend on weather reports from the airport, which is closed, due to the weather. Whether we will be able to give you the weather tomorrow will depend on the weather.*

All clear now?

*. . . . . . . . . . . . . . .A glance through the pages of the* Prestwich
Guide *reveals the following planning application: 235
Hayward Road, Change of use. Aquarium to fish and chip
takeaway . . . . . . . . . . . . . . . . . . . . . . . . . . . . . . . . . . . . . . . . . . . .*

★ ★ ★ ★

# Getting It Taped

When Canadian photographer Peter Duffy was sent along to
cover the unveiling of a plaque at City Hall, St George, British
Columbia, his blood did not exactly race in his veins. In short, the
prospect bored Duffy stiffer than the cold.

He decided to brighten an otherwise dull afternoon by taping
a nude picture over the plaque. He then replaced the drape and
stepped back to await developments, as the official party
advanced on to the rostrum.

Let the splendid Duffy himself tell
the tale. 'The Mayor did not see
the picture at first. Then he did
and his mouth just hung open.
Instead of the usual ripple of
applause, there was absolute
silence. Then I was sacked.'

# *You Ought To Be In Pictures*

At the time of the De Lorean scandal, photographers of the *New York Daily Post* were ordered to proceed with some haste to the Manhattan home of Christine, dishy wife of the disgraced car-maker.

This was no easy task for the eager snappers. Not surprisingly, Mrs De Lorean had little or no desire to perform before the shutters and flashes, and remained doggedly out of sight.

Eventually, after many hours of waiting around, the Press gang espied a mysterious-looking woman, well wrapped up against the autumnal chill. She hared out of the building and leaped into a chauffeur-driven limo. A photographer broke from the pack and raced across the sidewalk after her, shooting rolls of film in her wake. The film was rushed back to the office, along with the photographer, who modestly awaited the acclaim to which he was entitled.

The executive could hardly contain their glee as the film was processed and the prints spread out on the editor's desk.

What they were looking at was an interesting selection of pictures of an obviously highly-miffed Mrs Rupert Murdoch, wife of their own employer, who lived in the same block as the De Loreans.

# Sorry!

There is little that is more noble than the sight and sound of a gentleman admitting that he was wrong, particularly when he is a gentleman of the Press.

On July 5, 1982, the American magazine *People* displayed a correction which stated:

> *The June 28 issue carried a story on a new diet product called starch blockers. On rechecking his tapes, reporter David Sheff has found he misquoted Dr John Marshall. Dr Marshall did not say that the writer Cameron Stauth was a 'dirty rotten scum who got greedy'. What he said was: 'He's an unscrupulous little (pause) gentleman.'*

Nice to have got that one cleared up, Dave.

# Name Of The Game

Gossip columnist Nigel Dempster was approached by racehorse trainer Alan Jarvis, who wished to name a yearling after the great man of the *Daily Mail*.

Colleagues advised Dempster to agree, citing a dreadful example of what could happen if he didn't.

Soccer manager Brian Clough was once asked by an owner for permission to give his horse his prestigious name. Permission was promptly refused.

The disappointed owner then dubbed the nag Blabbermouth instead and was last seen cantering away chuckling in a vengeful manner.

★　　★　　★　　★

..............*Spanish police on duty guarding the honeymoon retreat of Angus Ogilvy and Princess Alexandra spotted a heavily perspiring British cameraman perched in a tree in a bid to obtain an exclusive. With total lack of Andalusian charm, they simply chopped down the tree......*

# *Eye, Eye*

The satirical magazine *Private Eye* is fond of making others the butt of its humour, but it is not often to be found on the receiving end itself.

So, when a prankster sent out a pile of false invitations to the magazine's 21st birthday party ball at the Reform Club, editor Richard Ingrams did not laugh immoderately. In fact, the only guffaw to be heard among the staff emanated from the convulsed culprit, Mr Paul Halloran.

As is only right and proper, Mr Ingrams exacted his full measure of revenge on the hapless hack. He informed the assembled staff that the cost of entertaining those invited by the hoaxer would use up all the cash set aside for the staff Christmas bonus.

There was much grumbling over this cheerless prospect, and Mr Halloran was plunged into a negative paddle area. The poor fellow suffered untold agonies of the damned for one full week before a savagely gleeful Mr Ingrams informed him that it was all a joke.

# *Garden Fate*

A free newspaper distributed in the Surrey area contained the following disconcerting advertisement placed by a local landscape gardening firm:

## DON'T KILL YOURSELF
## IN YOUR GARDEN
## LET US DO IT FOR YOU

# Angus Ogilvy, Ace Reporter

Jounalists are often frog-marched out of Royal establishments, but it is not often that royal personages are mistaken for hacks and dealt with accordingly. It happened to the Hon. Angus Ogilvy, whose regal association is by way of marriage to Princess Alexandra.

When in Spain with his wife, Angus arrived late for an engagement with King Juan Carlos and Queen Sophia. At the gates he asked the police: 'Is the English princess here?'

Much to his astonishment he was seized and dragged off to the nick, accused of being an interloping reporter.

And there he remained until Alexandra popped along to have him freed.

# Palace Revolutions

They're changing guard at Buckingham Palace – and not before time, it would appear.

Only days after Michael Fagan dropped in unannounced in the Queen's bedroom to ask for a light, two dreadful cheeky fellows from the *Daily Mirror* set out to test the authorities' claim that no such breach of security would ever happen again.

After a few friendly pints in the palace local, reporter John Merritt and photographer Peter Stone obtained an official parking permit from a palace gateman.

Armed with this valuable document, the newsmen were able to go in and out of the Royal Mews entrance at will.

They were even invited to sit in a royal coach scheduled, only a couple of days later, to carry the Queen to Westminster for the State Opening of Parliament.

When challenged with this further slackness, a palace spokesman dismissed it as 'absolutely an administrative matter', saying, 'I do wish people would stop calling it a security thing.'

Probed by, inevitably, a *Mirror* reporter as to whether staff were being questioned about the episode, the official continued: 'With a security matter like this, *of course* we are investigating.'

# First With The News

Don't believe everything you read in the newspapers is not a piece of advice you would need if you had happened to be in Chicago on Presidential election night, November 2, 1948.

Thomas Dewey was red-hot favourite to win and the *Chicago Tribune* was so confident that it printed its first edition story of his triumph before the results started to come through.

## DEWEY DEFEATS TRUMAN

screamed their banner headline in enormous front page capital letters.

Maybe the *Trib* knew something the rest of the country didn't, but Harry S. Truman was later properly revealed as a landslide winner.

The editor needed the aid of a trowel, if not a shovel, to get the egg off his face before popping along to the proprietor's office to explain how it all came about.

# Read Letter Daily

A letter was printed in the letters column of the Paris edition of the *New York Herald* on December 27, 1899.

Enquiring about the relative merits of the Fahrenheit and Centigrade temperature scales, the reader's query seemed innocuous enough.

Imagine his surprise, therefore, to see the same letter, word for word, on the next day's editorial page.

The *Herald's* proprietor, James Gordon Bennet, also spotted the slip-up and was so livid that he decreed that the letter should be published in every single issue of the paper for the rest of his lifetime.

6,700 issues later, the old curmudgeon died – and we still don't know if the writer ever received a satisfactory answer!

# Bread Sales In The Sunset

The people of recession-hit Tyneside are on the breadline in a very big way. Or so the fraternal comrades in Russia are led to believe by Vladimir Skosyrev, London correspondent of *Izvestia*.

He reported to his horror-struck native land that youths in Newcastle upon Tyne and its capitalist-oppressed environs were made to slave for 60 hours a week, without even so much as a break for lunch. Not that they could have afforded lunch even if the opportunity had presented itself.

Vladimir really had tears as big as bumper plates rolling down Russian cheeks all the way across the vast steppes with his account of the old and unemployed queueing for hours on end outside a baker's shop in the city in the hope of coming away with a cut-price stale loaf, or even two if it was a really big day.

The shop involved in this outrage was Greggs, the classiest bread emporium in the area. Mr David Parker, the firm's managing director, thought the whole thing was hilarious.

He said: 'One of our 70 shops sells day-old bread or mis-shapen cakes at half price. I think most of our customers buy in bulk for their deep freezes. I think we'll have to open a shop in Moscow.'

# Better Late...

In July 1969, the lofty *New York Times* apologized to Professor Robert Goddard for maligning him 49 years earlier. The newspaper had ridiculed the space pioneer for suggesting that a rocket could function in a vacuum.

Nearly half a century later Apollo 11 proved the prof. absolutely right.

Donning unaccustomed sackcloth and ashes, with a hair shirt on the side, the *Times* said:

> *It is now definitely established that a rocket can function in a vacuum.* The Times *regrets its error.*

# Hackademics

A recently established postgraduate course in journalism was staunchly defended by university authorities when the idea for it was announced to a barrage of taunts and criticisms from academics ('not a subject which readily lends itself to this type of in-depth academic study') and those 'untrained' practitioners of the trade who constitute the British Press ('who do they think they are anyway?').

The university's enthusiasm and confidence proved somewhat misplaced, however, when in 1982 it was revealed that 24 out of the 25 graduates attending the course had fallen at the first hurdle.

They had failed to pass the preliminary shorthand test.

# Bathload Of Boloney

Many journals, books, government publications and even some encyclopedias erroneously include a totally fictitious account of 'America's first bathtub'. The author of this farcical 'history' was the famous American humourist, H. L. Mencken.

The whole saga began with the December 28, 1917 issue of the *New York Evening Mail* in which Mencken detailed the supposed purchase and installation of the first tub in 1842 by one Adam Thompson of Cincinnati. Allowing his zany imagination free rein, he went on to describe the incredible adventures of the bath – how it was banned by law by the health department, permitted only on prescription in Boston and subjected to a horrendous tax levy in Virginia. All-in-all, the whole story was a veritable Colossus of nonsense.

However, to Mencken's utter astonishment and considerable glee, the great clean-living American public did not see it that way. They believed every word of the ridiculous piece – and apparently continue to do so, in spite of the fact that an immediate and full retraction of the fable was printed in the same newspaper the very next day.

# Body Language

*.................. Errors concerning the world of medicine.....................*

# Mind How You Blow!

Coal-mining is a job that can easily get up your nose. So thought young miner Ronald Cutler in 1942 when, having just finished a shift at the Oakdale Colliery in Monmouthshire, he blew his nose to get rid of the clogging coaldust. To his surprise and consternation, as he blew, his eye fell out! Ambulance men managed to replace the eye on the way to hospital and the young man was later able to go home none the worse for his strange experience.

# Mum's The Word!

18-year-old Sharon Fox went to bed with a stomach ache one evening after gobbling a bag of crisps. The following day, however, was really crunch time, for the pains got worse until finally an ambulance was called. Half an hour later, Sharon gave birth to a 7lb daughter.

'I was amazed,' said the young mother. 'I'd no idea. I didn't have any morning sickness, cravings, or even a lump in my tummy. I spent the whole nine months in my usual size 10 clothes.'

# Reader's Digestion

The strange eating habits of a Canadian woman proved medically unfortunate when she was diagnosed as suffering from poisoning caused by a specific type of mercury, used in paper-making.

Every day for the last twelve years, she told incredulous doctors, she had eaten a box of tissue paper, and a cigarette pack, a bland diet spiced up by the occasional paperback novel.

So beware – a *consuming* interest in anything may be a fatal mistake!

# Taking Steps

Although doctors are not *always* right, it is undoubtedly true that it can be unwise to disregard their warnings – even from the most laudable of motives.

Take the remarkable case of Samuel Flecknoe.

For four years he had been paralysed and unable to walk. Then one Sunday in 1913, when 'something' told him to get up, he obeyed the impulse, and set out to make up for lost time.

On the Friday, 32-year-old Samuel walked down to a matinée at the local theatre, returning home with a full programme of fun mapped out for the following day.

Cautionary words from doctors were waved aside. Young Samuel was determined to take up his bed and hop, skip and jump.

Pride comes before a fall, they say, and it was when he refused his anxious brother's assistance in climbing the stairs that night with the words 'Leave me. I'll carry *you* if you like' that he made his big mistake.

For at the top of the stairs he stumbled and fell all the way down, landing unconscious at the bottom.

He was out cold for several days and, on coming to, decided to learn from his crash course in remedial therapy and remain in bed until his recovery was complete some weeks later.

# The Flickering Lamp

Florence Nightingale, the fabled Lady With The Lamp, was convinced that her own flame of life was about to snuffed out. After returning from the Crimean conflict in 1856, she managed to get about for another year before taking to her bed to await the dread footfall of the Grim Reaper creeping up the main staircase. She was consumed with the notion that she had a terminal heart disease and that her life 'hung by a thread which could snap at any second'.

In the event, the 'thread' proved more like a cast iron chain and failed to snap until the old nurse was knocking 91, having spent her last 54 years as a self-imposed semi-invalid.

# Ice Scream

A flood knocked out the power and damaged the emergency generators at the Smith Hospital in Fort Worth, Texas. The absence of power had put paid to the air conditioning and the entire hospital was becoming something of a hothouse. With confusion reigning all around, a young psychiatric patient took charge, passing himself off as a medical official.

He sent a team of highly-trained staff on a search for ice which lasted all through the night.

A hospital spokesperson admitted later: 'We finished up with 2,000lb of dry ice in the lobby.'

She added that no one had thought for a moment to question the authenticity of the young fellow at the helm because 'Well, he seemed to be doing such a good job'.

# What A Corker!

A Somerset man had been deaf in one ear since the age of three. Many years later he was visiting a new doctor, who decided to have a look at the offending ear. To the GP's utter amazement, a cork suddenly popped out and hit him in the eye.

The patient explained calmly: 'I must have put it in there when I was a lad.'

# Living Death

A contender for the Freakiest Funeral Of All Time must be the mournful event at the Rumanian town of Moinesti, when the bereaved became unnerved, not to mention hysterical, at the sight of the dear departed lady's anxious face peering down at them from the open coffin as it was carried across the road to the graveyard.

The whole thing became altogether too much for them when the 'corpse' leaped out of her box and legged it down the road – straight into the path of an oncoming car, which killed her.

# Toxic Shock

Lonely widow Dora Ashbough carried poison in her purse for 20 years, in case the world became too much for her. That day came in 1930, when Dora was 71 and almost destitute. She swallowed her poison and lay on the steps of the University of San Francisco to await death. In her hand was a note saying:

*I leave my body to the university for medical purposes.*

The university was obliged to delay taking up her kind bequest, for Dora was not dead. The poison she had carried around for two decades had lost its lethal powers.

# Well, Strike A Light!

A man was admitted to the Intensive Care Unit of a North London hospital, suffering from a serious chest ailment. He was placed in an oxygen tent and soon began to make a recovery.

However, as an inveterate cigarette smoker, the man soon became desperate for a fag. Nurses and doctors constantly warned him of what would happen, but the stubborn smoker erroneously thought he knew best.

One day he managed to smuggle in some matches and a packet of Silk Cut. He lit up – and with an ear-splitting bang, patient and oxygen tent exploded in the same instant.

# Ears A Funny Thing

Retired tailor Harold Senby had never been happy with his hearing aid. For one thing, it had never seemed to work very well or do him much good. In the 20 years he had worn it, his hearing did not seem to have perked up at all.

He discovered the reason for its inefficiency when, at the age of 74, he went along to Leeds Hospital for a check-up. Incredulous doctors gently broke the news to their patient that for all those years he had been wearing the deaf aid in the wrong ear.

# Hard Centre

Doctors responsible for the opening of a new phobia centre in Derby should perhaps have considered more carefully the nature of the condition they were seeking to treat before launching such an expensive venture. As it was, it did not take long for lack of attendance to draw attention to the error.

'The trouble is,' said the organizer, 'many phobia sufferers are frightened to come to the centre.'

Elementary, my dear doctor.

# Unkind Cut

July 21, 1907 was definitely a day to remember for railway porter Johann Kovacs, valued employee at the station at Bihar, Hungary. Poor Johann collapsed at work as a result of humping a particularly difficult trunk. He was taken to the local hospital where the doctors pronounced him very dead indeed. They then decided to hold a post mortem. Johann's body was stripped and laid on the dissecting table, whereupon the pathologist turned to the assembled group of medical students and announced, 'I shall now make the first incision.'

So saying, he bent to his labours, but at the first prick of the scalpel, Johann woke up with a start. It took him a few seconds to become fully aware of the awfulness of his position, after which he made a heroic effort to assault the amazed surgeon. It took several doctors to restrain him.

# First Sign Of Madness

A sign which was put up in a hospital corridor was taken down again after only four hours. It read:

## DEPARTMENT OF PSYCHIATRY – ROUND THE BEND

# Slim And Unhappy

Dieting was the undoing of garbage collector Ruffs Jackson. He was very fat indeed; so fat the refuse collection authorities in Chicago ordered him to lose a gargantuan 200lb or be fired.

Ruffs single-mindedly went on a crash diet, suffering the usual agonies of the damned until the target was reached. Unfortunately, his dieting endeavours left him so weak that he could no longer lift the garbage bins and he was fired for inefficiency.

The very same day, his wife left him because she could not stand her new-look husband.

# Unlucky Break

Toddler Andrew Bewell fell down the stairs at his home in Hebden Bridge, Halifax and broke his right ankle.

He was whisked off to Halifax Royal Infirmary to have treatment.

But when he came home his *left* ankle was in plaster.

Not even his parents noticed the clanger until bed-time when the swollen, unplastered right ankle was obvious for all to see.

So the following morning a red-faced casualty department received another visit from the unfortunate youngster.

# Splashing Out

The 11-year-old son of an East London family had an unusual medical problem. Not only was he a regular sleepwalker, but during his somnambulatory wanderings he often put the plug in the bath, started the taps running and then went back to bed, leaving the family in the flat below to discover what had happened when the water began to drip through their ceiling.

This soggy habit cost the boy's family hundreds of pounds in repairs over a period of time.

When, in desperation, they consulted their doctor, he prescribed the immediate confiscation and concealment of the plug – and considered the problem easily solved. But he was very wrong. The mistake revealed itself when a cascade of water descended into the flat below. Undefeated, the sleepwalker had used the plug from the basin and returned to his old trick!

The parents were so disappointed and so reluctant to face their downstairs neighbours, whom they had reassured would not be troubled in this way again, that they asked a local radio disc jockey to apologize for them.

This was duly done. For good measure – though perhaps a little unfortunately – the DJ chose to play some 'mood music' – a record of Bobby Darin's old hit, *Splish Splash*.

# Wrong In The Tooth

The Greek philosopher Aristotle may have been a great thinker, but when it came to medical knowledge, he left much to be desired. He believed throughout his life that men have more teeth than women, whereas, in fact, there is no difference.

It is known that Aristotle was married twice, but nothing is known of his wives' dental status!

# Nun Nicer

The cure for the common cold is home-made rhubarb wine, according to the nuns of the Poor Clare convent in York.

The nuns have been producing the rhubarb tipple for around 100 years, but they never realized its medicinal properties until they stopped making it in order to economize. Suddenly they all started coming down with colds and chills, but soon recovered when the wine-making was resumed. The magic tipple was on sale at £1.50 a bottle and news of its sniffle-fighting possibilities led to a run on the brew. This in turn excited the interest of the Revenue men, who warned the sisters that, although the proceeds went to charity, the whole thing was illegal.

Sounds like a lot of rhubarb.

# Lost Leaders

................... *Errors concerning politics and politicians* ...................................................

# A Whopper Of A Majority

When President Charles King of Liberia offered himself for re-election in 1928, the voters were so enthused by the prospect of another Kingly term that they gave him a thumping majority of 600,000 over his opponent, Thomas Faulkner.

The colossal nature of this defeat was something of a puzzle to Mr Faulkner. Not surprising, since the total electorate of Liberia numbered less than 15,000 at the time!

# Taverne In The Town

On a walkabout during the 1982 by-election at Peckham in South East London, would-be SDP mould-breaker Dick Taverne stopped an old man in the street and asked if he recognized him. The voter perused the elegant, Chelsea-based QC for a few moments and then responded: 'Aren't you Dick Turpin?'

A few days later it was highway robbery all right as the Labour candidate, Harriet Harman, romped home ahead of the luckless Taverne.

# The Wrong Arm Of The Law

The legendary Mayor of Chicago, Richard Daley, not exactly known for his liberal attitudes, went on record to defend the brutality of his police force during the infamous Democratic Convention in his city in 1968.

He declared: 'The police are not there to create disorder. The police are there to *maintain* disorder.'

★    ★    ★    ★

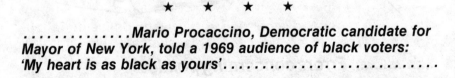

. . . . . . . . . . . . . . *Mario Procaccino, Democratic candidate for Mayor of New York, told a 1969 audience of black voters: 'My heart is as black as yours'.* . . . . . . . . . . . . . . . . . . . . . . . . . . .

★    ★    ★    ★

# Classic Loser

Horatio Bottomley (1860-1933), one-time MP for the London constituency of South Hackney, was also a journalist, financier – and notorious swindler.

On one glorious occasion at Blankenberg racecourse in Belgium he tried to put one over on the bookies. Entering six of his own horses in a minor race, he gave the compliant jockeys detailed instructions on the order in which they were to pass the finishing post.

Having placed his bets, Bottomley retired complacently to the grandstand to watch a satisfyingly large bundle of banknotes gallop happily past.

In the event, however, neither he nor anyone else was able to watch much at all, as a thick swirling mist rolled in from the sea just as the race got under way. The bribed jockeys lost sight of one another and crossed the line in anything but the prescribed order.

Bottomley, in his usual fashion, lost a small fortune, adding another to his long line of 259 bankruptcy petitions.

# Hail Hailsham!

The awesome majesty of the Palace of Westminster has been known to stir the soul of the most ripped-off tourist, but never more so than in the dank and dreary November of 1979.

Lord Hailsham, the Lord Chancellor himself, was strolling across the lobby of the House of Commons when he saw Neil Marten, a Tory MP and long-standing friend.

Hailsham, ever attentive to such details, recalled that it was Marten's birthday and gave an imperious wave to his friend, as he called out: 'Neil!'

A troupe of camera-clad tourists crashed to their knees as one.

★　　★　　★　　★

.............*The eager and enthusiastic police at Sabah, Indonesia, prevented 138 communist sympathizers and other potential trouble-makers from entering the country. They identified the radical hordes of aliens because, as they put it, they all looked suspicious and 'wore red ties'*..........

# By George

George Thomas, the former Labour Cabinet Minister who became one of the great Speakers of the House of Commons, was out canvassing on the doorsteps of his beloved Wales one day, when the door was opened by a lady clad in mourning.

Mr Thomas, who was once President of the Methodist Conference, uttered a few words of condolence and was then ushered into the parlour where he found the deceased laid out.

After a few moments of properly respectful silence, the lady in mourning told her famous visitor: 'Granny would really have appreciated this, you know. She was dead Labour.'

# Grave Allegation

Gerald Ford, who often found great difficulty in walking around without hitting walls or falling over, was as good with words as he was with budget figures. He once delighted onlookers, not to mention the scribblers of the media, by declaring: 'I say that if Abe Lincoln was alive today, he'd turn over in his grave.'

# Oh, Grattan

Irishman Henry Grattan (1750-1820) was a man who deserved to have his name writ large in the annals of parliamentary debate as the only man ever to lose a motion that enjoyed unanimous support.

Addressing the House on his theme of the day – precisely what it was is lost in the mists of time – Mr Grattan found to his great pleasure nothing but approving nods and murmurs from his fellow Members. It was when it came to formulating a written motion to be nodded through that things began to go wrong for poor Henry. He took so long to arrive at a form of words that the House began to get restive.

Finally, an opposition Member suggested that, instead of a formal motion, the Government Minister concerned should give a verbal assurance of support. Henry, by this time covered with confusion, agreed. The other MPs, however, did not and so, on a technicality, the motion was lost.

# Sung Of Praise

Kim Il Sung, President of North Korea, certainly has a way with words. Blowing his own trumpet with whole page ads in all the British national newspapers a few years ago, detailing the potential of his beloved country, was obviously very exciting. But, like all great men, the President also has to undertake less blood-stirring engagements.

During a visit to China, Sung was invited to inspect the methane-generating units of Sichuan Province. (The gas is produced from fermenting human and pig dung and straw. This yummy mixture is an excellent source of energy and can also be used for cooking – a really mouth-watering prospect.) Sung was terribly impressed by the whole thing.

'That's very good,' he enthused, going on to say, somewhat (we hope) misleadingly: 'We in Korea have all the right ingredients in great abundance.'

History does not relate what kind of reception awaited the President when he returned home to the people of whom he apparently held such a *high* opinion!

# Bombing Out

One of the perils of attending the annual season of political conferences is the blizzard of leaflets, pleas and assorted battle cries from well-meaning groups. One such piece of paper, thrust upon delegates to the Labour conference at Blackpool, was from the Jobs Not Bombs youth marchers. It said: 'If the power of the Labour Party and trade unionists is fully mobilized then nuclear disarmament can be stopped.'

# Now You Hear It, Now You Don't

Addressing an audience of GIs about to be shipped out to Vietnam in 1966, President Lyndon B. Johnson announced that his great-great-grand-daddy had perished at the Alamo. This was a nice line to hand those perhaps about to perish for their country. It was also a complete, copper-bottomed lie, as the world's Press, which was covering the event, would surely find out. LBJ'S aide pointed out that a scandal would follow the remark. Johnson gazed at him and replied: 'I never said that.'

The aide swallowed hard and told him that he and everyone else had heard him say it. Johnson snorted. 'I don't give a damn what you heard,' he said. 'I did not say it. I can state categorically that my great-great-grandfather did not die at the Alamo.'

There was no scandal.

# Madam Chairperson

Anarchy was brewing at the headquarters of the Amalgamated Union of Engineering Workers in Peckham, South East London, as leaders brooded over ways to bring Mrs Thatcher's government to its knees.

They must have thought that Mrs T. numbered ESP among her many phenomenal attributes when they walked into their top secret meeting room to be confronted by...the Iron Lady herself, seated in the Chair, bearing a look of glacial disapproval.

Several of the brothers began to murmur vaguely apologetic

and self-exonerating words until one, less short-sighted than the rest, revealed to them their mistake. Some joker had placed a lifesize cardboard cutout of the PM in the chair.

Seizing probably the only chance they will ever have of overthrowing the premier, the brothers with one accord picked up the offending cardboard personage, and threw her unceremoniously from the room.

★　　★　　★　　★

*. . . . . . . . . . . . . .Josef Stalin, the infamous Soviet leader, not noted for his humanitarianism or uproarious humour, remarked in 1933: 'Gaiety is the most outstanding feature of the Soviet Union' . . . . . . . . . . . . . . . . . . . . . . . . . . . . . . . . . . . . .*

★　　★　　★　　★

# Two Stars For Amazement

There's a small hotel in the historic town of Chester and if its owner, Bill Whitelaw, ever wished it was well and truly on the map, he must have thought his wildest dreams were about to come true when a letter arrived from the top men at the American Embassy in London.

Mr Whitelaw's quiet, away-from-it-all retreat, which boasts eight comfy bedrooms, costing a mere £13 a night all-in, was block-booked for a Mr Reagan and 19 heavies from the secret service... Could it be? Surely not *the* Mr Reagan...

Bill, aged 56, was further amazed when a letter confirming the arrangements dropped on his door mat. It also insisted on a command post and special security outside the Reagan bedroom.

However, the tingle of excitement Chez Bill was dimmed more than somewhat when the red-faced Americans admitted that they had erred. They had somehow managed to confuse Bill's humble but homely Gloster Hotel guest house with the Grosvenor Hotel, where the top people stay when they are in town. The Mr Reagan involved did not even turn out to be Ronnie, but only his 36-year-old son, Michael, who was on a European tour along with his wife and son. And the 19 bodyguards.

# Individual Interpretation

When Mr S. Seymour, a State Department interpreter, accompanied ex-President Jimmy Carter on an official visit to Poland, he helped create a situation more reminiscent of Whitehall farce than the dignified behaviour associated with official East-West diplomatic relations.

The scene went as follows:

Carter: (to bored but polite gathering of 500 Poles) When I left the United States...

Seymour: (spontaneously 'translating') When I left the United States never to return...

Sudden interest among audience.

Exchanged glances of disbelief.

Carter: (oblivious) I understand your hopes for the future...

Seymour: (relentless) I know your lusts for the future...

Dawning realization among Poles.

Giggles.

Carter: (desperately worried) I have come to learn your opinions and understand your desires...

Seymour: (delightedly) I desire the Poles carnally...

The story is still told with some glee at embassy parties the world over.

Less gleeful was the response of the US Press Secretary, who remarked coldly of the event, 'It was not a good translation. There will be a new translator tomorrow.'

# Thinking Ahead

Mr Arthur Lewis, Labour Member of Parliament for Newham North, stood up in the House of Commons on October 18, 1982 and made a ringing call for improved redundancy payments for MPs. This was unwittingly sensible of him, for, very shortly afterwards, his local constituency party shocked him by deciding not to reselect him as their candidate at the next General Election.

★　　★　　★　　★

..............*The great Lloyd George made a fool of himself at the 1919 Versailles Peace Conference, when he told the Italians to boost their banana crop as a means of reviving their economy. He was rewarded with much Latin glowering and muttering, for, of course, Italy does not grow bananas.........................................*

# Expert Timing

Sir John Hoskeyns, the former head of the Prime Minister's élite Policy Unit, was due to speak at a lunchtime fringe meeting at the 1982 Tory conference. Unfortunately, he failed to turn up. Shamefaced, he later admitted that he had got the dates all mixed up.

Sir John is the man who used to advise Mrs Thatcher on such momentous matters as the precise timing of elections.

★  ★  ★  ★

*. . . . . . . . . . . . . .One of the greatest gaffes in the history of diplomatic relations occurred at a grand dinner held at the White House in honour of the Egyptian Ambassador, when one of President Carter's aides turned to the ambassador's wife, grabbed at her bodice and informed her: 'I always wanted to see the Pyramids'. . . . . . . . . . . . . . . . . . . . . . . . . . . . .*

★  ★  ★  ★

# Follow My Leader

President Calvin Coolidge (of whom Dorothy Parker remarked on hearing of his death, 'Why, I never even knew that he was alive') invited a bunch of his hick friends to dine at the White House. It was one of his first social evenings after his election.

The friends, not having the remotest clue how to behave in high society, had an informal council of war beforehand and decided to copy Coolidge's actions down to the smallest detail.

All went well until dinner was over.

Then the President, who perhaps had more of a sense of humour than his friends suspected, solemnly tipped half his coffee into his saucer and added cream and sugar.

Following the prescribed formula, the friends duly followed suit.

They then froze in consternation and embarrassment as Coolidge calmly placed the saucer down on the carpet for his cat.

# Coffee And A Dash

Conservative Member of Parliament Michael Brotherton was most anxious to get to Grimsby (stranger things have happened) to pay a surprise visit to a Dr Barnado coffee morning. But, as so often happens to those relying on British Rail, his train from London did not enable him to make the vital connection at Newark, Nottinghamshire.

Nothing daunted, a resolute Mr Brotherton, who sits for Louth, Lincs, called on the services of no less than three police forces.

First, police at Newark drove him to the Lincolnshire border, whence a second patrol car sped him onward to the outskirts of Grimsby, where a third police car waited to take him to the actual coffee morning venue.

Unfortunately, by the time he made his way through the door, the public, which included some of his constituents, had all gone. Mr Brotherton later insisted that the three-car journey was absolutely necessary and he added: 'People love to see their MP.'

★    ★    ★    ★

*. . . . . . . . . . . . . .Nguyen Co Thach, the Foreign Minister of Vietnam, seems to be something of a whizz at economics. He was able to make this proud boast to an appreciative audience: 'We are not without accomplishment. We have managed to distribute poverty equally'. . . . . . . . . . . . . . . . .*

★    ★    ★    ★

# Load of Rubbish

A crowd of 250,000 earnest demonstrators turned up in Washington in 1978. They were there to celebrate Sun Day, a happening designed to raise the national consciousness of non-polluting solar energy.

Their cause was not overwhelmingly aided by evidence of their own slightly less than outstanding pollution-consciousness in leaving behind them 10 acres of ankle-deep litter and garbage, gleaming and glittering in the non-polluting sunshine!

# What's That You Say, Mr President?

In spite of his well-known experience as a film actor, President Ronald Reagan is still more than capable of fluffing his lines, with hilarious, and sometimes embarrassing, results:

### Ronnie the Peacemaker
In 1975, while still riding that long trail which led from Hollywood to Washington, Reagan told a gathering: 'The United States has much to offer the Third World War.'

Assuming from the stunned and attentive silence this remark engendered that he was on to a winner, the White House hopeful repeated the line no fewer than nine times during his speech.

### Ronnie the Broadcaster
Waiting to address the American people over the Polish Government's decision to ban the free trade union Solidarity, President Reagan obliged the sound engineer with a few well-chosen words. Not for him the 'testing, testing, one, two three, four' of lesser beings; he launched straight into what was uppermost in his great presidential brain: 'My fellow Americans, yesterday the Polish Government, a military dictatorship, a bunch of no-good lousy bums...'

Needless to say, due to 'human error', these admirable sentiments were heard on trannies from coast to coast.

### Ronnie the Historian
One day President Reagan and his good lady were patiently awaiting the arrival of royal guests. America's leader had prepared a welcome address to greet King Olav and his queen. Fortunately, someone rather better schooled in recent European history was on hand to save the President from a disastrous gaffe: the Queen of Norway died in 1954.

RONNIE IN BLUNDERLAND

# Truth, And Other Lies

George Smathers was a man who believed in the truth – in the broadest and most flexible sense of the word. A truly fearsome right-winger, Smathers was out to defeat and destroy his Liberal opponent, Claude Pepper, during the 1950 US Senate primary elections in Florida. To achieve this end, without swerving one iota from his guiding principle of honesty, he hit on a brilliant scheme.

Relying on the limited vocabulary and unlimited impressionability of the voters, he revealed to them that Pepper was 'a known extrovert, with a sister who is a thespian'.

As this bombshell sunk into the thick skulls of the populace, more shock horror revelations swiftly followed. Pepper's brother was mercilessly but quite accurately exposed as 'a practising *homo sapiens*' while Pepper himself could be proved to have 'matriculated' at college. The real clincher was the appalling news that the beastly Pepper went in for 'celibacy before marriage'.

The hick voters out in the sticks reacted just as Smather knew they would, mistaking this catalogue of unexceptionable attributes for evidence of intolerable and disgusting debauchery, and the 'foul fellow' was soundly beaten at the polls.

And *that's* the truth.

# For The Record

Those who heralded Reaganomics as the unerring road to renewed prosperity and balance for the ailing US economy may be beginning nervously to wonder where they went wrong, as it appears to be proving more of a twisting lane towards a dead end.

By the year ending 30 September 1982, overspending had risen to a colossal £65,294 million.

This was almost twice as much as that achieved under the previous record-holder (Gerald Ford) and is confidently expected to rise to a staggering £120,000 million before the end of Reagan's term of office.

# King Arthur

The problem of naming streets is one that besets town councils the world over. The worthy citizens of Selby in Yorkshire are no exception. When they opted, among others, for 'Scargill Rise', they felt no sense of impending disaster. It sounded inoffensive enough.

However, they reckoned without the activities of the Yorkshire miners' leader, Arthur Scargill, whose elevation to national chief suddenly made the innocuous side road sound like an intentional tribute to the great man.

Sensing the danger of a press 'exposé' and aware that public opinion was not in favour of Mr S., councillors decided to retrieve their error, and the name was withdrawn.

But the spokesman who announced this compounded the mistake. Explaining that the council wished to do nothing that could be understood in any way as implying political bias in either direction, he went on to fall very heavily off his elected fence by stating that the name had been dropped in order 'to make miners moving to the area feel more welcome'!

★　　★　　★　　★

............*Viscount Montgomery, speaking in the House of Lords, dismissed the aims of the 1965 Homosexuality Bill with the following remark: 'This sort of thing may be tolerated by the French, but we are British – thank God'*........................................

★　　★　　★　　★

# Suckered

Herbert Hoover, whose very name implies a great ability to deal with hot air, told a waiting nation in 1928: 'We in America today are nearer the final triumph over poverty than ever in the history of the land.'

So near and yet so far. Within only one year the American Stock Market collapsed and the nation went bankrupt.

# Plains Speaking

When President Reagan visited the vast farmlands of Illinois, his aide led him to anticipate a crowd of some 8,000 eager rural voters. When only a quarter of this number turned up, Ronnie turned an accusing eye on his over-confident aide.

Red-faced and blathering, the young man tried to cover his blunder, but only succeeded in achieving a further one by asserting that 'the farmers did not want to get their tractors muddy.'

He was unable to explain to the President how the farmers managed to preserve the pristine cleanliness of their machinery when ploughing the dirt soil from which they obtained their livelihood!

★　　★　　★　　★

. . . . . . . . . . . . . . *A Democrat running for Mayor of New York in 1968 delighted his rivals by describing his appeal in the following attractive terms: 'Frank O'Connor grows on you, like a cancer'. . . . . . . . . . . . . . . . . . . . . . . . . . . . . . . . . . . . . . . . . . . . . . .*

★　　★　　★　　★

# Non-Stick Mud

During the American presidential election campaign of 1884, the Democratic candidate, Grover Cleveland, was the victim of a smear campaign.

Having discovered that the unmarried Democrat was the father of widow Maria Halpen's son, the Republican camp rushed out a series of leaflets. Beneath pictures of the illegitimate offspring was printed the caption: 'One more vote for Cleveland.'

But the whole dirty trick backfired with a satisfying crash.

Cleveland decided on the highly unusual political course of telling the truth. He admitted the dalliance, and its results, and threw himself on the mercy of the sensible and forgiving electorate.

Much to Blaine's chagrin, the voters decided that they quite liked a man with a naughty secret, particularly when he had the decency to admit it, and Cleveland was duly elected.

# Hung Vote

Seven Members of Parliament who missed a vote on the Transport Bill in October 1982 explained later to their respeotive aggrieved Whips that, far from being a deliberate revolt, their non-appearance was all a ghastly mistake, ironically caused by a bit of trouble with their chosen method of transport: they were stuck in a malfunctioning lift at the Commons.

# Out Of His Own Mouth

One of ex-President Richard Nixon's most memorable blunders (apart from getting found out!) during the notorious Watergate scandal, occurred during a nationwide TV broadcast. Attentive viewers were astonished to hear the confident assertion: 'this is a discredited President.'

The mistake was soon made clear. Rather than an accurate description of his own unenviable position, Nixon had actually intended to object against the use of unfair legal *precedent* in the case against him. At least this unwitting shaft of honesty caused some members of his audience more amusement than most such speeches were to do.

# Looking Glass

The go-ahead PR men of the Labour Party decided to install a 'magic glass' prompt machine for Michael Foot's rallying speech to the 1982 Conference at Blackpool. This device is designed to enable a speaker to appear to be speaking off the cuff, while in fact reading a cunningly reflected version of his speech off a specially constructed disguised mirror that stands before him like an innocent piece of protective glass.

Just in time, party chieftains examined the contraption and stepped in to prevent what could have been a disastrous (though hilarious) mistake. They pointed out that Mr Foot's somewhat erratic freestyle of movement while on the platform would inevitably result in him knocking the whole thing over – to the imminent danger of those faithful seated in the first few rows.

# True Blue Blush

A prospective Conservative Parliamentary candidate was out canvassing one evening. He became lost in the narrow back streets of the town and wound up in the red-light district.

Still in a state of blissful ignorance, the young hopeful rang the nearest door-bell, which happened to be that of a 'house of ill fame'.

When the door opened the confused canvasser realized his mistake and could only splutter that he was from the Tory party.

'Never mind, love,' was the encouraging reply, 'you're all the same to us. Come on in.'

# Seeing Stars

................... *Errors concerning*
*film and TV personalities* ...............................................

# Crossed Wires

When Ken Hughes was directing 89-year-old Mae West in
*Sextette*, he encountered a delicate technical problem. The
ageing star was unable to keep up with the constant changes in
the script, so, eventually, a bizarre solution was developed.

A small radio receiver was concealed in her wig and her lines
were relayed to her by Hughes just before she was due to speak
them.

As solutions go, this was not a great success. First, other
actors were disturbed by hearing Hughes' voice emanating from
the wig, giving answers to lines they had not yet delivered.

Then, by some radiophonic mischance, a police helicopter
tuned in to the wig wavelength, and the entire company was
brought up short when, during a passionate love scene, Miss
West delivered the unforgettable line: 'Traffic on the Hollywood
Freeway is bogged down.'

# What's In A Name?

When actor Joel McCrea decided to go freelance after his MGM
contract expired, Sam Goldwyn threw a lavish lunch party for
him, with some of the greatest names in the business seated
around the table. He rose to his feet to address the gathering.

'And so we say goodbye to my good friend Joe McCrail...'

An embarrassed aide leaned across, tugged his chief's
sleeve and muttered: 'Sam, it's McCrea...'

Goldwyn glowered down on him and hissed: 'For seven years
I've paid him $5,000 a week and you're trying to tell me his
name?'

★　　★　　★　　★

. . . . . . . . . . . . . *Actor George Raft was not perhaps a great
judge of potential box office success. He refused the leads
in* High Sierra *and* The Maltese Falcon, *in the latter case
because he did not wish to work with an unknown and
unsung director – John Huston!* . . . . . . . . . . . . . . . . . . . . . . .

★　　★　　★　　★

# You Must Remember This, Or

# Maybe You'd Rather
## Forget

The film *Casablanca* made Humphrey Bogart and Ingrid Bergman immortal, for when it is shown on late night TV it regularly keeps up more people than overspiced curry.

It would have been very different, however, if the producers had had their way.

First choices for the roles, Hedy Lamarr and George Raft, turned down the parts – and doubtless kicked themselves all the way to the bank.

# Bird Brains

The 1939 movie *It Ain't No Sin* was to be a big money-spinner for Paramount Studios and they wanted to give it the full publicity treatment.

An eager, and definitely imaginative, publicity man hit on the bright idea of shutting a platoon of parrots in a room with a record that played the name of the film over and over again. Quite soon Paramount were the owners of a flock of feathered friends which could squawk 'It ain't no sin' to order.

By this time, however, the studio bosses had changed the name of the picture to *I'm No Angel*.

# Novel Attitude

Hollywood story editor Jacob Wilk was given an advance look at the galley-proofs of a forthcoming novel, for which the publisher had high hopes. He was so impressed that he rushed right in to see his boss, studio chief Jack Warner, and urged him to take up a $50,000 exclusive option on the available film rights.

To Wilk's dismay, Warner refused, saying: 'I wouldn't pay 50,000 bucks for any damn book any damn time.'

The book so confidently dismissed was Margaret Mitchell's *Gone With The Wind*.

# Way Out West

Mae West was a sex goddess of the silver screen for more years than most people would like to remember. By the time she made her last movie, the legend and the star were both coming apart at the seams.

She was 89 when shooting started and was hardly able to move or hear. But she was still surrounded by a team of hangers-on who tried to tell her all the things they thought she wanted to be told.

'Miss West, you are wonderful, just wonderful,' they drivelled. 'Your skin, your face, your hair are in a class beyond compare. You don't look a day older than 29.'

Mae West drew herself to her full height and treated them to the famous bedroom drawl: 'Thanks fellers, I'm supposed to be 26.'

# Taylor-Made Gag

Laurie Taylor is Professor of Sociology at York University. He is also well known for his acerbic wit, as displayed on such programmes as BBC Radio 4's *Stop The Week*.

This should have been enough to alert the thoroughly nice and unsuspecting people concerned with the Thames Television afternoon programme *A-Plus*. But, perhaps working on the principle that no one does anything wicked before teatime, they allowed themselves to be taken for something of a ride by Prof. Taylor.

Luring the programme's researchers to York with tales of a remarkable band of Arab musicians called El Moruhci, Taylor proceeded, along with his six accomplices, to adorn himself in authentic Arab garb and create what he hoped was the genuine Arab sound. So impressed were the Thames TV minions that they roared back to London full of their exciting find.

The pranksters duly appeared on the show the following week and, with the aid of giggling convulsions from the venerable professor, gave presenter, Kay Avila, the runaround.

Nina Burr, the producer, putting a good face on it, later observed: 'They certainly fooled us – but it made a very funny item.'

# Abandoned Hope

Bob Hope found himself in the unaccustomed role of being on the receiving end of the cold shoulder one evening at a grand reception at the US Embassy.

A senior British official, failing to recognize the world-famous comedian, displayed less than the requisite diplomatic grace when he turned his back on Mr Hope in mid-anecdote and strode purposefully away.

The celebrity was not surprisingly offended. It is not known whether he whispered something of his pique into the ear of his friend, Mr Reagan, who was also present, or whether embassy walls really do have ears.

But at any rate it is rumoured in diplomatic circles that the poor humourless Brit is paying for his *faux pas* – perhaps by playing an unenviable part in *The Road to Siberia*!

# Calling The Tune

Frederick Loewe, composer of the music for such famous shows as *My Fair Lady, Brigadoon* and *Camelot,* threw a lunch party in Hollywood one day. When the food was delayed by a crisis in the kitchen, Leowe filled the waiting minutes by playing a selection of his best-known numbers on his grand piano.

Among the guests was Sam Goldwyn, who was most appreciative. Afterwards, he patted the composer on the back and told him: 'You know, Fritz, you've got a few possible hits there.'

# Double Agent

In the far off days when Lord Grade was still plain Lew, a theatrical agent on his way to fame and fortune as a TV and movie tycoon, he made it a practice to visit London shows in search of bright new talent.

On one such occasion he was much excited by a double act which was clearly destined for greater things. After the show he rushed backstage, warmly congratulated the two and told them that he would make them big stars if they signed up with his organization. The performers agreed that it was time their career took a new and more lucrative turn. But, they told Grade, he would have to get things sorted out with their present agent.

'And who is that?' Grade asked.

'Lew Grade,' they replied.

# Gloria In Transit

Gloria Swanson, star of many silent movies and later sensational in *Sunset Boulevard*, took unto her a husband, one Marquis de la Falaise. Miss Swanson's mother congratulated her daughter on the event and then phoned her lawyer to ask: 'What the hell is a markee?' The lawyer told her: 'It is one of those things that they hang up in front of a theatre. It is intended to keep the rain off the customers.'

This was too much for Mother. 'Christ,' she wailed. 'Gloria just married one of those things today.'

# Ballou Ballyhoo

Kirk Douglas was originally offered the classic role of Kid Shelleen in *Cat Ballou*. His agent talked him out of it, on the grounds that he should not allow himself to appear as a comic drunken gunfighter. It is not known whether Mr Douglas sent a congratulatory telegram to Lee Marvin, who won an Oscar for the role. Or what he had to say to his hapless agent.

# A Quiet Laugh

Conrad Nagel, heartthrob of the silent days, once observed that silent pictures were a great source of merriment for deaf people everywhere. As expert lip-readers they were, he pointed out, able to understand *exactly* what the actors were saying to each other, which often had very little to do with the story in hand.

Nagel always denied the oft-quoted tale of the film in which he picked up a girl, carried her to the bed and leered down at her, only to hear her say: 'If you drop me, you bastard, I'll kill you.' He maintained that it was another actor, who was slightly unwell by virtue of a massive hangover, who tried to lift the actress. She told him: 'Why don't you just use your breath? It's more than strong enough to do the job.'

All of which had the deaf rolling in the aisles, to the total bewilderment of everyone else in the house.

# The Age Of The Cable

The impudent journalist who sent a telegram to Cary Grant's agent inquiring:

HOW OLD CARY GRANT?

was mistaken if he thought his cheek would go unnoticed, or unpunished, by the great star. Having opened the cable himself, Grant telegraphed back:

OLD CARY GRANT FINE. HOW YOU?

# Harty Cheers

Russell Harty, of TV chat show fame, was not surprised to receive an invitation to present the prizes at the annual Mr Hardware contest. Mr Harty, who frequently gets similar approaches from all sorts of organizations, was at the time taking part in the Black Pudding of the Year Award ceremony in the same town, and so agreed readily enough.

Supposing it to be an Ironmonger of the Year event, or some such extravaganza, Mr Harty went along to the venue at a popular disco in the city expecting a dull but uncontroversial evening. To his surprise and growing discomfiture, he soon found he had made a ghastly mistake. Not only was there not a single ironmonger to be seen, but he found himself having to judge between five effete-looking young men, each of whom wore the teeniest pair of tiny briefs and one of whom sported for good measure a pair of authentic-looking handcuffs!

The title of the competition, it later transpired, had little or

nothing to do with hammers and nails, but was taken from the name of a '*potent* medicine' sold in shops of a certain rather dubious nature in the city's red light district.

# Proper Charlie

One-time Hollywood comedian Jackie Vernon was a childhood fan of Charlie Chaplin. Like all good supporters, he wrote countless letters to his idol. Unlike most, he did not get a single reply.

Many years later Vernon was, by chance, in London at the same time as Chaplin, who had come out of retirement to direct Sophia Loren and Marlon Brando in *The Countess From Hong Kong*.

As fate would have it, Vernon happened to be in a restaurant on the same night as the ageing Chaplin.

He simply could not resist walking over to the great man's table.

'Please excuse me,' he said. 'You won't know me, but I am one of your greatest fans. My name is Jackie Vernon.'

Chaplin looked up and replied: 'Tell me, why did you stop writing?'

# Spot The Insult

When Hollywood producer Arthur Hornblow Jr had a son, his colleague, the legendary Sam Goldwyn, called to congratulate him.

Hornblow thanked him and revealed that the new arrival was going to be christened Arthur Hornblow III.

Goldwyn pondered this with puckered brow.

'Why Arthur?' he asked. 'Every Tom, Dick and Harry is called Arthur.'

# Common Interests

Groucho Marx, the fast-talking, cigar-chewing leader of the famous Marx Brothers comedy team, once confessed to an unfortunate mistake made during a prolonged courtship: 'Many years ago I chased a woman for almost two years, only to discover her tastes were exactly like mine: we were both crazy about girls.'

# 24 Carat Goldwyn

At the time when he was completing his 'great production of *The Best Years of Our Lives*, top Hollywood producer, Sam Goldwyn, was invited to make an appearance on Bob Hope's radio show.

He asked screenwriter Harry Tugend to give him a gag for the occasion. Tugend suggested that Bob Hope should say: 'How are things going since I left your studio, Mr Goldwyn?'

The producer was to reply: 'Since you left, Bob, we've had the best years of our lives.'

Goldwyn was delighted with the idea, and with the plug for the film. Sadly, where Goldwyn was concerned, there was many a slip twixt script and lip.

He was so pleased that he told his associates: 'That Harry Tugend is a very clever man. He wants to have Bob Hope ask me how things are since he left MGM. Then I've got to say, "Since you left things are better than ever".'

# Into Cattle

Celebrated horror film producer Alfred Hitchcock was most upset to read himself misquoted as having said that 'Actors are like cattle'.

Hurrying to rectify the error, he rang the newspaper concerned. What he had actually said, he told them, was: 'Actors *should be treated* like cattle.'

# He Never Said That

James Cagney, the famous gangster-movie actor, is one of the most impersonated of all stars of the big screen.

Yet even the President of the United States, in his own very creditable Cagney impression, uses the mistaken expression 'you dirty rat'.

In fact, in all his many gangster films, Cagney never once used this world-famous phrase.

# Works Of Heart

.................. *Errors concerning romance and marriage* ..................................................

# Unlucky In Love

One of the unluckiest lonely hearts of all time must be the 22-year-old Los Angeles man who advertised through the personal columns of a magazine for a woman to accompany him on the vacation of a lifetime in South America.

His ad struck at least one responsive chord, for he received a quick reply. From his widowed mother.

# Aisle Be Seeing You

Irishman Albert Muldoon was delighted and honoured and charmed to be best man for his dear pal Christopher at the tiny church in Kileter, County Tyrone.

Unfortunately, the beauty of the occasion was altogether too much for him and he stood on the groom's left instead of on his right. The priest, not knowing either of them from Adam, duly put the questions to Albert, who responded by taking the time-honoured vows.

The awful truth emerged, to be sure, but only when the happy triple were involved in signing the register. A second ceremony was immediately held and this time the bride managed to leave on the arm of the right man.

In this case, fortunately perhaps, the best man did not win.

# Rib-Tickling Romance

Anna Mitlow, known for miles around Minneapolis for her beauty, did not mind having a kiss and a cuddle with her boy friend, but when his affectionate squeeze cracked two of her ribs, she felt things were going a bit too far.

The bonny Miss Mitlow took the unfortunate young man to court, asking for $30 damages, plus $1.50 for her doctor's bill. The judge told her: 'I'll give you judgement for the doctor's bill, but as regards the other $30 – well, a good squeeze like that is worth $30!'

I need hardly add that the case was brought back in 1930, long before the days when feminism would have made the old boy think twice.

# Happy Landings

Vera Czermak, housewife of Prague, was bitterly unhappy and depressed, for she had discovered that her husband was having an affair. She decided that the only answer was to end it all, and hurled herself from the window of their second-floor apartment.

She landed on Mr Czermak, who chose that moment to arrive at the main entrance to the building.

He was killed, but Vera survived.

# Fat And Happy

Linda Leiro put an ad in her local newspaper at Wimborne, in Dorset:

*Wedding ring for sale. Hardly used.*

Anxious relatives and friends beat a path to her door to see if anything was amiss. But 29-year-old Linda was happily able to tell them that her marriage was not on the rocks. Far from it.

She had been on a diet and had shed so much of her chubby old self that her gold band kept falling off her new slimline finger. Husband Alberto, with true Latin chivalry, dashed into town and bought her a new one.

Then Linda got fed up with her diet and began to nibble the odd biscuit, cream cake and plate of pasta again. The weight came rolling back, 20lb of it, and so did the old wedding ring. The new one was by now far too small. So she put it up for sale.

'I'm very happy,' she said.

# The Very Odd Couple

Appearances can be deceptive, as the neighbours of an ordinary-seeming couple were to discover. When Mr and Mrs O. arrived in town, she was pregnant. The local council granted them a flat, and everyone was happy.

But all was not what it seemed. For, far from being just another ordinary working couple Mr and Mrs O. were, in fact, both women!

'Mr.' O, who dresses in men's clothing and likes to be called Ossie, has lived with her friend for more than four years. They wanted nothing to complete their happiness other than a family. When conventional adoption proved out of the question, they disliked the idea of artificial insemination and so they found 'a tall, handsome candidate with a nice personality', who duly obliged.

The couple's neighbours were astonished that they could have failed to notice when their mistake came to light some time later, but it did not materially affect their feelings towards 'such a nice young couple'.

# In The Picture

In 1936, Lady Beddoe Rees enthralled a women's afternoon meeting at Romsey in Hampshire with the tale of a young couple who thumped on the front door of the local cinema manager in the middle of the night.

They told him they had left 'an article of great value' in the cinema. The manager opened up the cinema and the great search was on.

They found their precious treasure where they had left it. It was their baby, still fast asleep on the seat next to where they had been sitting.

Lady Rees assured the audience that the story was true and persons of title are not given to telling tall stories, are they?

# Catty Response

A couple in the Michigan town of Ypsilanti were arguing so loudly and vehemently that the local police were called in by the neighbours.

The forces of law and order discovered that the couple had been fighting over possession of the cat.

Sadly, the said cat had expired somewhat abruptly, due to being pulled asunder in a tug-of-love between the two combatants.

# Which Is Switch?

A double wedding was about to take place in Saudi Arabia in 1978.

Unfortunately, the Moslem father of the two brides mixed up the names of the grooms and sent his daughters on the journey into matrimony with the wrong partners.

For several days the unhappy man attempted to set matters right, but the two girls told him not to bother about it.

They declared that they were very happy with the way things had turned out.

# Thirty Years' Solitary

After 30 years of marriage, a 60-year-old North London woman decided she had made a mistake, and sued for divorce. When the appeal was granted, her husband was devastated. He told the judge he thought the marriage had been 'fairly happy.'

I suppose it depends on how you look at it.. during all those years, the man had kept his wife a virtual prisoner in her own home, allowing her out for half an hour each day to do the shopping, locking up the telephone and only allowing her to see other people in his presence. Moral: do not confuse absence of complaint for presence of contentment.

# On The House

A recently-published survey on marriage carried out by a women's magazine reveals a startling misconception among us enlightened 'liberated' males! While stating the apparently shocking statistics that only one in three husbands makes any sort of token effort at helping with the housework, while one cad in ten does absolutely nothing at all, the magazine also shows that most wives are quite happy with this state of affairs.

53% said they actually *enjoy* doing the household chores. So – all of you who cry loudly about exploitation and the downtrodden housewife – you're *wrong*!

# Hell Hath No Fury...

An airline pilot who decided to jilt his longstanding girlfriend should have chosen a better time to do it. Announcing his intention just before a round-world flight, he asked the girl to return some of his belongings to his flat. When he returned to his flat, the pilot found his 'phone off the hook. Puzzled, he picked it up and listened. A tireless American voice chanted: 'At the tone it will be three twenty-six and ten seconds.' The jilted girlfriend had dialled the Transatlantic speaking clock, and notched up a bill running well into four figures!

# Change Partners

If you look forward to an exciting wedding night and are a self-employed shop-keeper, do not arrange to marry during the run-up to Christmas. The bride of a couple who made this mistake found herself spending her five-night honeymoon with – her mother-in-law!

Admitting that the timing had been unfortunate, the young husband yet made his position abundantly clear: 'Business comes first. If you don't make money, you just can't live.'

Luckily for him, his young wife says she gets on very well with her mother-in-law and that they had 'a lovely time'. She did add, however, a little ruefully, that her new husband 'was rather unromantic'.

# Only Human

*.................. Errors concerning misjudgment*
*and foible .................................................................*

# Dead Loss

Church treasurer Angus Duncan came up with a raffle prize that the lucky winner really could take with him when he went. In addition to such fripperies as a colour television and an electric toaster, Angus offered a free funeral.

His aim was to raise £500 for the Baptist Church in the Worcestershire parish of Feckenham. Tickets said that the booby prize was a 'non-transferable' voucher for the £9 church funeral fee. But the local people took a very grave view of Angus' little wheeze and sent the tickets back.

Pub landlord Brian Grub was one of those who refused to sell the 50p tickets. He said: 'There are many elderly people in this area. Just imagine if they had won the funeral voucher. We would have felt awful.' And Betty Leek, from the village Post Office, said: 'It was very tasteless and not at all the thing to do.'

A somewhat cowed Angus said: 'It was all meant to be a bit of a joke, but obviously people have not got my sense of humour. Luckily I had only sold 40 tickets and when all the trouble started I was able to make sure that people got their money back.'

★　　★　　★　　★

*. . . . . . . . . . . . . . In 1979 a Spanish Air Force ace managed to shoot himself down: his bullets ricocheted off the practice target in the Iberian hills, and then hit his jet, forcing him to eject to safety – and ridicule. . . . . . . . . . . . . . . . . . . . . . . . . . . . .*

★　　★　　★　　★

# Mouse That Roared

Adolf Hitler was a man with a lot of ideas, and most of them bad. One of his dafter schemes, designed to assist the Nazi effort towards world domination, was Project Mouse. Mouse was intended to be a battleship that confined itself to the land.

It was 50 feet long, with a 1,500 horse power engine, armour plating thick enough to withstand attack from a tank, and enough fire power to be most unpleasant. As befits a battleship, it was watertight and could get across rivers underwater.

Dr Porsche, who worked for Volkswagen and later found his niche in life with sports cars, was the designer of this monstrosity. In 1944 he sent the Mouse forth on a series of road trials. The series was very short, for the 180-ton monster ploughed up and ruined the roads, damaged the foundations of buildings it passed and, when it left the roads, simply sank into the ground. Along with the whole project.

# Start The Day With A Bang

Danny Arnold, the gun-toting sheriff of Bexar County, Texas, was not best pleased when he missed his breakfast because his alarm clock went off three hours late at his London hotel.

He dressed hurriedly in traditional style – frock coat, fancy waistcoat and gunbelt – and then strode purposefully into the reception room where 129 guests were enjoying morning coffee.

To announce his arrival, he pulled out his .38 Smith and Wesson and fired it at the ceiling. Although the gun was loaded with nothing more alarming than blanks, the smoke activated the fire alarm bells at the Heathrow Sheraton Skyline.

Sheriff Arnold shook his head later, as he mused: 'It only took a couple of minutes for the whole place to be surrounded by fire trucks and firemen. I immediately apologized to everyone for ruining their coffee break. I never guessed that firing a gun would cause so much trouble.'

# Down To A Tee

When the great American baseball player, Babe Ruth, challenged champion golfer Walter Hagen to a sociable eighteen holes, he made a grave tactical error. For Ruth seemed able only to maintain his game for half that number.

The explanation was simple. It takes about the same length of time to play nine holes of golf as it does to get through a whole baseball game. So established was the timer in Ruth's mind that it clicked off after its normal span, and that was the end of his concentration – and his game of golf.

# How The Royal Melbourne Drove Into The Rough

The Royal Melbourne Golf Club is quite the snobbiest in Australia. But it very nearly bunkered itself forever and, with stunning timing, chose the week in which it staged the Australian PGA championship to do it.

At the time, well-intentioned officials were attempting to raise cash for improvements by disposing of an acre of wasteland to a local developer. Sadly, the committee worthies were far more adept at reading the run of the greens than maps and plans and suchlike. It was only when the builder, Mike Warson, applied for planning and development permission that he discovered that he was the owner of 60 acres, including the 8th, 9th, 10th and 11th fairways on which such stars as Ballesteros and Miller were playing.

The value of the land was $20 million, a hundred times the sum Warson had actually paid out.

He said: 'We all had a good laugh at the club's expense.'

But, a sportsman and certainly a gentleman, he got the Royal Melbourne out of a very nasty hole by returning the land.

# Artistic Licence

The Metropolitan Museum of Art in New York has made a few expensive mistakes in its time.

In 1918, for example, it paid $40,000 for an ancient Etruscan statue. One arm was missing, and the thumb of one hand was gone.

It was not until 1960 that one Alfredo Fioravanti came forward to confess that he and five other men had actually made the statue 50 years before.

He produced the missing thumb to prove it – it was a perfect fit!

# Damn Dam

The massive May Dam near Konya was intended by the Turkish Government as the incredibly expensive answer to local irrigation and other watery problems.

It looked really impressive, but the whole project turned out to be totally useless, for the engineers responsible seemed to know little about geology. The huge reservoir created by the dam sat inconveniently on extremely permeable alluvium and karstic limestone. More than 30 sink holes formed, thus allowing all the gathered water to drain away into the ground.

# Chess Congestion

A commercial artist, seeking to fire the infant population of Britain with his own enthusiasm for the ancient game of chess, produced a nifty little book called *The Amazing Adventures of Dan the Pawn*.

Dan is depicted as the hero of the piece, picked by the White King as his champion in the battle with the 'Black Army'.

Sadly, the artist reckoned entirely without the vigilance of the National Union of Teachers' official organ, *Teacher*.

The journal lashed into the book, accusing it of 'subtle racism'. The reason for its ire was that the white pieces defeated the black.

# Dishonesty Is A Real Drag

A teenager went with his mother to the county court at Blackburn, Lancashire. Once there he nipped into the ladies and changed into his sister's clothes, adding a touch of realism by stuffing his socks into the bra to look like breasts. His mother then duped court officials into handing over £931 held in trust for her 17-year-old daughter.

The disguised boy told officials that 'she' was emigrating. The town's magistrates, who later heard them admit obtaining the cash by deception, thought the whole thing was a drag and gave the pair suspended jail sentences.

# The Computer Kid

Gilbert Bohuslav loved computers, chess and Western novels. He had already taught his brainy computer, the DEC 11/70, to play chess with him, and the next step was obvious.

Gilbert, who worked in the computer department at Brazosport College, Houston, Texas, fed DEC 11/70 with the most-used words in every Western he had seen or read.

Then he sat back, eagerly awaiting the outpouring of his electronic J. T. Edson. And this is what he got:

*Tex Doe, the marshal of Harry City rode into town. He sat hungrily in the saddle, ready for trouble. He knew that his sexy enemy, Alphonse the Kid, was in town. The Kid was in love with Texas Horse Marion. Suddenly the Kid came out of the upended Nugget Saloon. 'Draw, Tex,' he yelled madly. Tex reached for his girl, but before he could get it out of his car, the Kid fired, hitting Tex in his elephant and the tundra. As Tex fell, he pulled out his own chess board and shot the Kid 35 times in the King. The Kid dropped in a pool of whisky. 'Aha,' said Tex, 'I hated to do it, but he was on the wrong side of the Queen.'*

Even making allowance for Gilbert's own sense of humour (elephant? tundra?) it was clearly time to go back, if not to the drawing board, at least to the chess board.

# Dash It All

A hyphen is a little thing, not even paramount among punctuation marks. It hardly ranks with the lordly full stop, or even the comma.

But it once cost the United States taxpayers no less than $18.5 million.

The day when the cash registers went wild was July 22, 1962, when Mariner 1, the Venus-bound rocket, had to be blasted into pieces as it suddenly surged off its ordained course.

The reason for this costly malfunction was that a humble hyphen had been left out of the flight computer programme.

# No Escape

The Fire Brigade at Barnsley in Yorkshire were proudly on full dress parade for the opening of their smart new headquarters.

The splendour of the occasion was somewhat diminished by the arrival of some factory inspectors, who had turned up to give the custom-built showpiece the once-over.

They immediately ordered one tiny little modification...to include a fire escape.

# Call Of The Wild

Paul White was exceedingly fed up, not to mention sacked from his job as car park assistant at Cambridge, Massachusetts, following a row with a lady driver. The irate woman had cursed him something rotten and left him with his ears burning at the abuse.

As a result of this episode, he decided to help all those suffering from an addiction to the same foul language. To this end, he founded Curseholics Anonymous and set up a round-the-clock hotline.

Unfortunately, he was obliged to scrap the whole idea – because he was getting far too many obscene calls.

# Just The Ticket

People duped into paying cash to a Birmingham con man for cars they were never destined to receive, little dreamed that their unjust mistake was designed, in the criminal's eyes, to further the course of justice. It appears that the man conducted the swindle in order to raise funds to pay for his appeal against a previous conviction to be heard at the European Court of Justice!

# Yela Peril

British soccer clubs, wistfully watching the World Cup on the telly, have often thought that the answer to falling attendances and standards might be the introduction of some Brazilian-style flair. Clydebank, the somewhat unglamorous Scottish League club, would be only too happy to point out some of the pitfalls of this course of action.

In 1967 they were able to boast the not inconsiderable services of the Brazilian, Ayrton Ignaccio. The fans duly turned up, eager to witness a spot of samba soccer, at Forfar. They were doomed to disappointment, for Senhor Ignaccio had to be taken off, shivering, long before the end of the game. He could not stand the ravages of the Caledonian cold.

# Great Scott

Animal-lover Scott Brant was, quite naturally, delighted when a puppy came loping over to him as he strolled in the pleasant night air near his home in Minnesota.

The friendly little four-legged fellow licked his hand and showed no inclination to leave, so Scott took his new friend home, gave it some milk, and even cooked up a hamburger. The cheerful little visitor finished its meal and, as pets will, went for an exploratory roam about the house. But Scott was most distressed when the bundle of fun began tearing up the furniture.

He telephoned a vet for advice. The vet immediately contacted the local zoo, which sent around two keepers to collect its missing four-month-old lion cub.

# Quiet Goes The Don

Australian Don Bradman needed only four runs during the Oval test in 1948 to achieve an unequalled average Test score of 100. Marching down the pavilion steps with calm assurance, the Don misjudged a ball and was dismayed to find himself, only seconds later, walking back, bowled for 0. How is the mighty's wicket fallen, went up the cry – and Bradman's average remained at 99.94, still the best in history by a long way.

# Better Red Than – No-One

The Russians' attempt to launch their own wine in Britain was beset by disaster. The wines, which are big sellers back in the USSR were vilified by British wine experts. 'Chateau KGB', a white sparkling vintage, was described succinctly as 'awful', while 'Ruby of Crimea' and the grim-sounding Krim were 'unbelievable'.

To make matters worse, Russian trade delegate Alexander Krivenko confessed (perhaps after a few too many of the perilous red) that the biggest motive for making the wine was to lure his comrades from their notorious addiction to their beloved vodka.

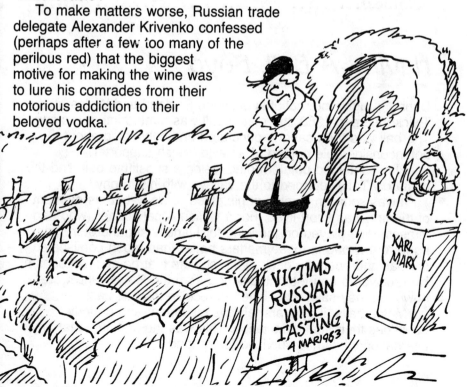

# Swan-Downing

When a body discovered in an Indiana lake was found to have bite marks on the left cheek, the local sheriff's deputies (exiles from Hazzard County perhaps?) put their none-too-well-endowed heads together. Their conclusion? The attack could only have been made by a large swan. Of course.

Looking through their files, they came upon a likely suspect. Described as 'big and tough', the 50lb swan was duly arrested by these gallant upholders of Law and Order. It was only when the case came to court that the lawmen realized they had goofed. Under US law it is not possible to indict a feathered suspect! Back to the drawing board, boys!

★　★　★　★

............*Absent-minded footballer Mark Wadsley was very surprised when he turned up for a match at Carterton, Oxfordshire, for instead of bringing his kitbag he found in his hand only a sack of potatoes!*........................................

★　★　★　★

# Having A Ball, Boyo

During a rugby international between England and Wales at Twickenham in 1960, the match ball was punted into the crowd. The ball was then caught, punctured and concealed about the not inconsiderable person of an avid Welsh supporter.

Play continued uninterrupted, using a substitute ball, and the dastardly Taffy returned to the valleys with his trophy.

It was soon on display at his place of work, but his moment of triumph was short-lived. For a vigilant local copper (who had himself once played on the wing for Llanelly and therefore knew right from wrong in these matters better than most) confiscated the ball and posted it back to the powers that be at Twickenham. He received a courteous thank you from the R.F.U. who were, however, they said, astonished to receive the ball back.

Match balls, it appears, always disappear and nobody questions their final destination. This was the first time that any international ball had survived for so long.

# Air Blackmail

Police got a flying start in a strange case of blackmail in Germany back in 1929. A mysterious parcel had been delivered to General Franz Pattberg at his home at Homburg on the Rhine. It contained a box holding a carrier pigeon. A note instructed the general to attach £250 to the waiting bird and then set it free. The penalty for non-compliance would be death itself.

This crafty plot was foiled by the general, who immediately demonstrated just why he had risen to the top of his chosen profession. He informed the police, and then arranged for a plane to go up and follow the unsuspecting pigeon all the way home. Aerial photographs were taken of the house where the pigeon settled and soon afterwards the villain was amazed to see the police swoop on him and drag him off to jail.

# Why The Ladies Blue Their Top

Porn movies, one of the weekly attractions staged by the management of a social club in Hexham, Northumberland, were the cause of a complaint from the members of the ladies' darts team which played at the club on the same night. It was not that the ladies objected to any sexist or exploitative element of the blue movies. They merely said that the appreciative reaction of the audience was putting them off their game in the bar next door.

# Mind Your Language

When a used car dealer decided to advertise his latest shiny new model as on sale for a knock-down price of 1,395 'bananas' (a local slang expression for dollars), he reckoned without the literal-mindedness of his clientele. He was very taken aback when a woman arrived offered him a deposit of twenty-five bananas – of the yellow, edible variety. The proprietor was reluctant to agree to the deal. But the determined woman took him to court and won her case.

Then, having delivered the outstanding 1,370 pieces of fruit, she drove away in the car.

What you might call a banana split!

# Prophet And Loss

Something for nothing is the lure that fills casinos and betting shops. Many punters are prepared to believe in anything, 'foolproof' systems, dreams, visions, the lot. Thousands of them came forward in Italy in 1926, eyes glittering with lire signs, when word got around that a crippled peasant named Torraca had foresight of the numbers that would be drawn in the national lottery.

Crowds besieged the home of the little limping prophet. He told reporters: 'My family, assisted by the hand of God, found the key to the lottery. The secret was divulged by my father on his deathbed. But he told me I must benefit only the people and must never enter the lottery myself.' Cables and express letters poured in from all over Europe and the United States, as emigré Italians begged for the numbers. Armed men stood guard outside Torraca's home to keep away the throngs.

At last the numbers were given and there was an immediate rush on the lottery ticket offices. One office manager was nearly lynched for keeping the anxious punters waiting. Many poor people sold their few possessions to raise money to buy tickets.

Come the day of the lottery, incredible to relate, not one of the miracle numbers came up. It was obvious why Torraca's dying father had told him not to buy his own tickets! The prophet was a complete dead loss. He was also missing, having wisely decided to leg it, crippled or not. The Italian Government, however, was naturally highly delighted. They had made millions on top of the usual lottery revenue.

# Game, Set And Match

The sounds of dissension and derision addressed to line judges and referees are now as much a part of the Wimbledon Tennis Championships as strawberries and cream or Dan Maskell.

When McEnroe made his famous outburst in the 1981 Championships the press and public opinion were united in their conviction that he was – to put it mildly – mistaken. Thanks to scientific tests inaugurated in the US soon after this event, it is now possible to show the truth of this beyond doubt.

During the tests, twelve professional coaches played against each other, watched by an umpire, the full complement of line judges and twenty spectators seated at strategic angles in the public seats. The humans' eye view was then compared with electronic and computer analysis of the play.

The results showed that the players were the lousiest judges of all. Even the ice cream seller would have done better. The best of all – by a long puff of chalk – were the much-abused 'pits of the world' themselves, the line judges. So – Messrs McEnroe, Connors and Nastase, among many others, please note – any further such disputes would be a *definite* mistake.

★　★　★　★

**. . . . . . . . . . . . . .** *It is obviously unwise to be too cheerful at work these days. An 18-year-old girl discovered the truth of this when her boss fired her – for laughing too much . . . . . .*

★　★　★　★

# Rock Off, Alf!

The Locarno ballroom in Birmingham was one of Alf and Mary's favourite haunts. And when the old place was transformed into a mixture of flashing lights and 3,500 watts of sound called The Powerhouse disco still they remained loyal. At least, they would have done if they had been allowed in. Alf, who is 48, and Mary, three years his junior, were amazed to be told to rock on elsewhere because they were too old.

The Mecca organization, which owns the disco, admitted that they had refused admission to 400 people because they were over 25. An official said: 'Young people don't like old folk at their discos. They don't want to go out and meet their mum and dad. They've probably gone out to get away from them in the first place.'

Someone up in the Mecca public relations department must have turned an even more violent colour than the disco lights when the papers carried the story. To show they were sorry, they hastily invited Alf and Mary back to The Powerhouse for their very own session, after which they were treated to free cocktails.

But they weren't all that sorry, for the 'Darby and Joan' couple still won't be allowed in on Saturday nights.

# Walkies!

An audacious burglar failed to effect illegal entry into a house at Darlaston, West Midlands. No doubt finding the garden shed too heavy to pick up, he nevertheless determined to steal something. Professional pride was satisfied, for he walked off with Laddie, the house's brilliantly alert guard dog.

# For It Is Written

When ancient graffiti were found on the roof of the Church of Saint Nicholas at Agschurch, in Gloucestershire, the vicar was so proud of the discoveries that he decided to put on an exhibition.

But he hastily withdrew one prospective exhibit when he realized it described the author's sex life in amazingly explicit and intimate detail.

# That's Dynamite

During the American Civil War, a certain high-ranking officer decided one day to blast a trench into the middle of a Confederate camp.

After the smoke had cleared, his men jumped cheerfully into the newly-created trench and, following their orders, careered along it towards the Rebel forces. They were brought up short, however, by the discovery that their esteemed leader had failed to think of providing a way out!

The Confederates were amazed suddenly to see their entire opposition presented to them on a plate – or rather in a 6-foot hole.

The commanding officer, it is said, went on to bigger and greater things, having followed the time-honoured custom of lighting the blue touch paper and standing well back.

# A Big, Big Problem

When the powers-that-be at Central Park Zoo in New York City came up with a spectacular plan to rebuild and refurbish the zoo, they thought they would have no problem in finding temporary homes for the animals while the necessary work was carried out. But they were wrong – at least in the case of their four-ton elephant, Tina.

They failed to take into account Tina's widespread reputation for being more dangerous than the muggers and villains who reportedly lurk behind every scrub bush in the Park. The huge elephant has a pronounced predilection for crushing her keepers' arms and charging at strangers.

Not the ideal house guest! At the time of publication, the zoo's plans still remain in the 'pending' file owing to Terrible Tina.

# Damp Squib

A History Museum in the North of England thought it would ring the changes and organize a different kind of Guy Fawkes celebration.

It advertised a special Victorian Bonfire Night. Tickets were sold and, come November, a large crowd gathered in the Museum grounds.

They lapped up all the authentic traditional goodies – faggots and peas, groaty puddings, real ale, etc.

But, as the evening wore on, the crowd began to get restive and finally downright annoyed at the non-appearance of the fireworks.

It was then that the Museum's directors realized they had made an unfortunate mistake. Although, as an abashed official announced, the Victorians never had fireworks, twentieth-century celebrators (especially when they had paid good money to attend) would not be satisfied by anything less. It seemed they were in for a rocket!

A quick-thinking custodian saved the day by slipping out and returning with his own private store of Catherine Wheels and Roman Candles. So finally honour, if not historical accuracy, was satisfied.

# Ill Wind

Setting up a show is a notoriously dodgy business. Lesson number one in the Unofficial Organizers' Handbook reads: always *secure* your exhibits.

Those in charge of an exhibition at a North Wales Country Park failed to observe this elementary point and regretted the oversight when gale force winds, sweeping down off the surrounding hills, knocked over an old tram which stood in pride of place in the grounds.

Lesson two in the Handbook reads: always site your exhibits with due regard to possible mishaps. The Welsh team failed on that one too: the falling tram, transformed into a colossal nine-ton metal projectile, demolished the new Interpretative Centre which stood nearby.

Bad show, boyos!

# Banking For Beginners

The imaginative head English teacher of a South of England comprehensive school reckoned without the zealous probity of his charges' parents when he introduced a distinctly unusual essay competition.

Pupils were invited to use plenty of imagination and write describing the perfect way to rob a bank. They were also given maps and plans (of an imaginary town) to assist in achieving the requisite sense of realism.

The headmaster was astonished, some days later, to receive a 'phone call from the local Chief Constable, who had been advised by an anonymous parent of a possible juvenile crime wave about to break in the area.

When the mistake was explained, the Chief Constable was understandably a little put out. He was mollified, however, when he received an invitation – to judge the bank-robbing essay competition.

# Foulke Hero

Everyone has a breaking point. This lesson was learnt – eventually – by one of football's greatest eccentrics, 6ft 3 ins 22 stone goal-keeper, Willie Foulke. When he arrived at Chelsea Football Club in 1907, he soon established a reputation for his antics on and off the field.

On one occasion this jolly giant stopped a game by snapping the crossbar in half. On another, he grasped a member of the opposing team in his hamlike fist and stood him on his head.

These minor breaches of sporting etiquette the lenient club manager decided he could countenance. But when fun-loving Willie felt like a little pre-match snack, entered the dining room early and ate the entire team's dinners before they arrived, he really overstepped the mark.

A football team, like an army, marches on its stomach. Willie paid for his error of judgement – and his gargantuan greed – by finding himself on the transfer list.

He moved to Bradford Football Club, taking with him an additional 4 stones in weight accumulated during his sojourn in London.

*. . . . . . . . . . . . .The Ayatollah's military leaders ordered aircrews to bomb American satellites when they appeared over Iran. . . . . . . . . . . . . . . . . . . . . . . . . . . . . . . . . . . . . . . . . . .*

★   ★   ★   ★

# Rouge-Faced With Embarrassment

The London firm responsible for labelling a consignment of French plonk called Vin Rude for sale to the United States were guilty of a gross marketing blunder.

The labels concerned showed naked couples enjoying a rather explicitly sportive romp – presumably inspired and invigorated by the brew contained within. The red bore the admonition: SERVE STARK NAKED; the white adjured: SERVE WITH A THRILL.

Having failed to obtain a single order from the upright (and sober?) wine-drinkers of the United States, a director of the firm finally concluded 'the whole thing was just too rude for the Americans'.

That sensible nation prefers its vin ordinaire!

# Dyeing Swans

The scene: London's elegant Savoy Hotel. The occasion: the birthday party of an American millionaire in 1905.

To give the celebration a unique flavour, the hotel arranged for its courtyard to be flooded and a silk-lined gondola for the thirty guests to float on the water. A hundred white doves were set loose and flew over the Venetian replica, swans swam decorously alongside and a baby elephant deposited the five-foot-high birthday cake on the steps above the improvised lake.

The success of this artistic occasion was somewhat marred, however, when the swans began to keel over with wild and blood-curdling screams, dying in obvious agony.

It seems that a chemical that had been used to colour the water a delicate azure hue had been poisonous and had turned the poor creatures a whiter shade of pale.

# Old King Cole

It is often a mistake to take unlikely-sounding statements at face value – especially if there is money involved and the speaker happens to be noted for his rather off-beat sense of humour...

At midday one bright spring day in 1910, a lorry broke down in the middle of the bustling Place de l'Opéra in Paris. Traffic ground to a halt, horns began to screech and Gallic tempers rose. The driver, however, quietly got out of his cab, lay down on his back and slithered under the vehicle to make the necessary repairs. 30 minutes – and a colossal traffic jam – later, he emerged, apologized calmly to the crowd of exasperated *gendarmes* who had rushed to the scene to cope with irate motorists, and drove away.

The man was, in fact, an Englishman, Horace De Vere Cole – the most notorious practical joker of the Edwardian era – who that night gleefully collected thousands of pounds from friends who had foolishly bet him that he could not lie flat on his back for half an hour at the busiest time in the busiest traffic centre in Paris.

No doubt the redoubtable Horace laughed all the way to the bank.

# Ye Olde American Import

Immigration officials at Ellis Island, USA, decided in 1921 to greet the steady influx of people arriving to build a new home in the Land of the Free by serving them with a 'truly American dish'. A nice idea. Unfortunately, they chose ice cream, which originated in France in 1670 and did not reach the shores of America until well over a century later.

# Moonshine

According to a survey conducted in 1969, over a fifth of the population of Morocco were unaware that man had set foot on the surface of the moon.

Over 50% of these angrily accused their questioners of trying to hoax them.

# Scent To Pot

Florida students were delighted one year during their Rag Week festivities to welcome the offer of a local police officer to show off his tracker dog's remarkable sleuthing ability.

However, somebody blundered in selecting the venue for the event, for when, having concealed ten packets of cannabis about the room, the officer let his sniffing side-kick off the leash, the indefatigable bloodhound came back with 11!

# Tripped Up

Holidays and holiday brochures are one area often responsible for anguish and dispute as the returning tripper complains that the sky was not so blue, nor the sand so golden as the brochure suggested.

Such complaints are usually dealt with in soothing tones, but the organizer of an Essex travel club is a definite exception to this rule. He received a letter of complaint from a bank manager who made the mistake of pointing out some shortcomings in his holiday to Portugal. The club organizer wrote back:

> As well as trying to improve our holidays, we are also trying to raise the standard of our clients. I'm afraid you do not come up to the mark and I should be obliged if you would make your arrangements elsewhere in future.

The astonished client commented: 'I was surprised at the tone of the letter. I've travelled with this firm many times in the past and have even written to them before, telling them how much I enjoyed my holidays. This time I complained about departure delays and the hotel food and I got this very rude letter.'

But the club man was unrepentant and adamant that his complainant could go and get sun-drenched with someone else.

'This man is a pompous ass,' he insisted.

# Boozed Off

The history of live theatre is littered with classic clangers and first-night fiascos. None more dramatic, however, than that which took place at the opening performance, in London in 1875, of a French comedy of manners entitled *Écarté*.

The first Act opened with a drinking scene and the misguided producer decided to inject a little extra sparkle into the performance by filling the glasses with real champagne rather than the usual cold tea or coloured water. Not surprisingly, the cast took full advantage of this unaccustomed generosity and many of them fell before the first act curtain did! The entire play was cancelled before the beginning of Act Two and all the box office takings were returned to the disgruntled audience. The show never reopened.

The *débâcle* might perhaps have been foreseen by a producer more familiar with the French language. Roughly translated, the world *écarté*, appropriately enough, means discarded.

# Killer Maiden

James Douglas, Earl of Morton, was proud of the recognition he received when he introduced a guillotine-like device called the 'maiden' into his native Scotland. He regretted it some time later, however, for he was himself beheaded by the cruel mechanism in 1581, after being convicted of complicity in the murder of Lord Darnley, first husband of Mary Queen of Scots, in 1567.

# As It Is Written...

A certain young Frenchman thought that he had pulled off the perfect crime in Boulogne in 1942. But he was – quite unforeseeably – wrong...

The young man concerned was the nephew of a rich landowner. Having received many affectionate letters from his benevolent uncle, the youth harboured great expectations of a substantial legacy. Being unscrupulous and impatient, however, he decided to hasten the processes of Nature and poisoned the old man. Leaving nothing to chance, the nephew then forged a will naming himself as sole beneficiary, using his own letters as a handwriting guide. He then sat back to gloat over his newly-acquired fortune.

Justice intervened, however, in the shape of the old man's housekeeper. She went to the authorities and accused the young nephew of forgery. She should know – for apparently her employer had, in fact, been unable either to read or write and, for nearly 50 years, the faithful servant had preserved his secret by 'ghosting' all his correspondence and business papers. Including, of course, the very letters on which the murderous youth's original hopes had been founded.

# Poetic Justice

In 1944 in Sydney, Australia, two young poets decided to engineer a hoax which they hoped would not only send up a pretentious *avant garde* literary journal called – believe it or not – *Angry Penguins*, but also ridicule the petty censorship that beset Australia at that time.

Stringing together words and phrases at random, they sent the resulting gibberish to the journal's proprietors under the guise of 'the complete poetic works of Ern Malley, who recently died in obscurity at the tragically early age of 25'. Deeply impressed, the editor published the 'poems' in a special edition of *Angry Penguins*.

As the hoaxers gleefully prepared to reveal the journal's blunder, things took a turn for the better, from their point of view at least, as puritanical police in South Australia confiscated the poems and arrested the *Angry Penguins* editor for publishing indecent material.

In the ensuing court case, the prosecuting detective directed the judge's attention to a reference in one of the poems to a man going about at night carrying a torch. 'There is a suggestion of indecency here,' he told the court. 'I have found that persons who go around parks at night do so for immoral purposes.' The great detective then turned to another of the gibberish verses. 'The word incestuous is used,' he declared. 'I don't know what it means, but I regard it as being indecent.'

The judge agreed, the editor of the journal was duly convicted, and only then did the two hoaxers (from a discreet and anonymous distance) reveal the true nature of this glorious series of errors and idiocies. Those concerned have been trying ever since to live it down-under!

# Another Flynn Mess

Cornelius and Evelyn Flynn are movie fans of many years' standing – or rather sitting. Nothing, therefore, seemed more logical when Evelyn presented Cornelius with a son in 1968 than that the lad be named Errol, in honour of their favourite swashbuckler of the past.

However, Errol now laments his parents' decision. 'It can be very difficult,' he says. 'Once a referee in a football match booked me. He didn't believe me when I told him my name and just thought I was being cheeky. And new teachers are always suspicious of me, while the other kids just giggle. I'm fed up with it.'

# Whoa, Tally-Ho!

Public Relations people at the Co-op probably thought they were on to a popularity-boosting winner when they loudly proclaimed their decision to ban fox-hunting over their many acres of farmland. However, they might have been wiser first to have checked up on the consistency of their public stand.

As hunt devotees were quick to point out, a hunting scene is depicted in glorious technicolour full cry on every plastic bag containing the Co-op's Cumbrian Loaf.

# Clangers And Mash

With uncharacteristic ineptitude, advertisers of a private health insurance scheme much vaunted during the 1982 National Health Service dispute chose the signature tune of the television series *M.A.S.H.* as background music for their 2-minute slot on commercial radio.

As many TV viewers will know, M.A.S.H. is set in an army hospital during the Korean War where patients are treated in extraordinarily ill-equipped and slaphappy circumstances.

Although popular on the screen, such treatment might appear less so if one were actually to be on the receiving end!

★ ★ ★ ★

*. . . . . . . . . . . . . . A female crossword fanatic seriously overestimated the extent of her husband's patience when she continually woke him up as she struggled with the final poser through the night. On the fourth such occasion, the overwrought husband strangled her to death. A court acquitted him on the grounds of temporary insanity. . . . . . . . . . . . . . . . . . . . . . .*

# Hair-Brained Fashion

In Spain in the mid-fourteenth century a new fashion suddenly sprang up among the aristocracy. Soon everyone was doing it – old or young, politician or fop, every man sported an identical long black false beard.

The originator of this curious vogue can scarcely have guessed what a terrible and disastrous blunder it was to prove. Soon nobody knew who was who. Debtors escaped recognition by their creditors and villains hid behind cascades of hair while the innocent were led helplessly away to prison. Wives failed to recognize their husbands – until it was too late, and the market price of hair rose to astronomical heights.

Finally, King Peter of Aragon himself stepped in and called a halt to this hirsute chaos. A law was passed with all due solemnity, expressly forbidding the wearing of false beards in Spain.

# Long Awaited News

National Westminster Bank Access cardholders were recently invited by an enterprising new wine company to enter a lucky draw competition. A note at the bottom of the announcement stated: 'The winner will be notified by telegram.'

He/she may be a long time waiting, since, as we all know (except, that is, for a certain wine merchant who shall remain nameless), the Post Office abolished the inland telegram in 1982.

# Record Blunder

Thomas Edison (1848–1931) is best-known for his successful invention of the phonograph, forerunner of today's gramophone. Less fortunate, however, was a venture launched by him in 1888 – the talking doll. Fitted with a tiny phonograph in its body, the doll could recite a dozen favourite nursery rhymes. Yes, it *should* have been a sure-fire winner.

But – after making several hundred of the dolls – Edison discovered he had goofed. His firm had apparently sold the rights to make phonograph toys to another company some years earlier. Edison was compelled to halt production and have the dolls destroyed. The few that were saved have since become collectors items and only two are believed to be still in existence.

# The Age-Old Problem

The United States is renowned for its prowess in sell-anything-to-anyone marketing techniques. One enterprising mail order firm company thought it had spotted a promising new target for its health and 'reinvigoration' products – the elderly. As an inducement they made an opening offer of a free book encouragingly entitled *Sex After Seventy*. After many complaints, they had to admit their error. They relaunched the campaign – still offering the same book. This time, however, it was printed in large type. Now, it was hoped, the old folk who had written in would be able to read the book with no difficulty.

# Monkey Puzzle

During the war which raged between France and England in 1705 the people of England were constantly warned of the imminent threat of invasion from across the Channel. When a small ship was wrecked during a storm off the North West coast of England, therefore, the locals were suspicious to say the least.

The sole survivor of the wreck was the crew's pet monkey, which was rescued by local fishermen as it clung desperately to some floating timbers.

When the creature arrived in the coastal fishing village, the citizens, who were simple souls unfamiliar with such hairy primates, did not know what to make of it. But as soon as the monkey began to gibber weirdly and wave its long arms about wildly they recalled the descriptions of French agents that had been circulated by the government. Of course, they concluded, this must be part of a dastardly French invasion plot. The poor ape was then summarily tried and executed as a French spy.

# Family Favourites

Fathers! Be warned: It may be a big mistake to allow a television set into your home.

According to a recent study at Michigan State University, given the choice of getting rid of the TV or their fathers, an astonishing 35% of four-and-five-year-olds opted to give dear old daddy the big elbow.

# Don't Keep It Under Your Hat

It seems increasingly that there are no lengths to which shoplifters will not go in order to get away with their pilfered goods.

From the lady who secreted a 4lb joint of meat and a tin of tuna in her bra to the man who attempted to stuff a chainsaw down the front of his trousers, the tales of felonious derring-do seem endless.

But one woman went too far recently at a huge American-style hypermarket. Seeking to smuggle a large frozen turkey through the checkout without paying, she made the mistake of concealing the bird on her head – under a large and much-adorned hat.

She collapsed before she had the chance to leave the store and was later admitted to the intensive care unit of a local hospital.

It seems she had suffered a stroke brought on by the sudden exposure of her brain to below-freezing temperatures!

# Gold Drain

Much was made of the impregnability of the new gold vault when the Bank of England moved into new premises in 1800. So that when a workman claimed that he could easily enter the stronghold undetected, the Governor of the Bank was so confident that he agreed to a wager of £2,000 that it could not be done.

Sure enough, however, when bank officials arrived the following morning they found a trap door open in the centre of the vault and the workman sitting patiently awaiting them. He explained to the horrified staff that one day, while undertaking some sewer repairs, he had come upon a ladder. On climbing it and pushing up the door to which it led he had found himself, to his complete amazement, gazing upon the massed hordes of England's gold reserves.

It was, indeed, fortunate for the Bank that the man was an honest fellow. The Governor, red-faced at this gross blunder, found his £2,000 wager a very small price to pay for such a narrow escape.

# Bra Bar

In these days of women's liberation and equal opportunity, the life of the male employer is fraught with pitfalls and traps. Take the boss of an accounting firm in Nancy in Northern France for example.

Productivity in his erstwhile profitable accounting business began seriously to fall off when his 'token' female member of staff began to appear at the office quite obviously not wearing a bra. It seemed that this particular round figure 'disturbed' the day-to-day figurework of the male staff.

When the worried men tentatively suggested to the liberated demoiselle a change in her lingerie habits, she flatly (if that word does not sound too inappropriate) refused. Driven beyond endurance, the boss fired her.

That proved a very costly mistake. For, even in that deeply paternalistic society, such blatant *cochonnerie* is frowned upon, and the woman successfully sued and presented her account for substantial damages!

# Braking Point

One of the most remarkable cases of 'mistaken identity' occurred of recent years in Pery, Ohio.

The chief of police was suffering from a severe shortage of manpower.

He did not have enough money in the budget to increase the force in the ordinary way, so he did the next best thing. He recruited a life-size tailor's dummy!

Every morning the dummy, which was dressed in full police uniform, was placed behind the wheel of a spare patrol car and left by the roadside. The citizens of Ohio were completely taken in.

Speeding motorists mistook the dummy for the real thing and, in the words of the delighted police chief, 'as soon as they see the car with the cop in it, they slam on the brakes and slow right down.'

He went on to reveal that 'this dummy is so convincing motorists have even been seen going over to it to ask for directions.'

★  ★  ★  ★

. . . . . . . . . . . . .*A nineteenth-century French construction company must win the all-time prize for perseverance – and incompetence. In their abortive attempts to build a canal across the isthmus of Panama between 1881 and 1889, they lost over £150 million and 20,000 men were drowned . . . . . .*

# One More River To Cross

During the American Civil War battle of Antietam in 1862, Major General Ambrose Everett Burnside was in command of a crack force of Union troops.

During a forced march, the Unionists came to a broad river. Burnside scratched his hoary old head and hit upon the brilliant wheeze of sending his men single file across the only narrow footbridge.

Unfortunately, this exposed them to artillery fire from the Confederates posted on the opposite bank. They couldn't believe their luck – it was better than a rifle shoot at the local fair, picking off the poor boys in blue one by one. It was only when he had watched the greater part of his force destroyed in this way that Burnside decided to examine the mighty flooding river at closer quarters.

It turned out to be less than 3 feet deep. The men could have forded it with ease, lived to fight another day *and* kept their powder dry!

# Texas Manger Rangers

When a Norfolk playgroup presented their 1982 Nativity Pageant, their audience was somewhat surprised to see the baby Jesus being visited in the stable by gun-toting cowboys!

It seems this novel interpretation of 'peace on earth and good will to men' was decided upon when the children declared they did not fancy dressing up as shepherds.

# Naughty Auntie

The august British Broadcasting Corporation is usually the very essence of propriety in its dealings.

It was, therefore, greatly embarrassed when the news got out that it had paid white extras five times as much as their black counterparts during the African location shooting of an important documentary series.

The programme concerned was *The Fight Against Slavery*.

# A Merry Dance

The RSPCA was hot on the trail of a hotel proprietor who had innocently been sending out a very jolly brochure advertising the Christmas holiday attractions his establishment had to offer.

The programme promised:

# 𝔄 mediaeval banquet, complete with wandering minstrel and dancing bear

Oh no you don't, said the local RSPCA and promptly sent around a gentleman in uniform to see about arrangements for the bear. The proprietor could hardly answer the officer's indignant questions without laughing.

He said later: 'We can only surmise that the apprentice chef, aided by a Brighton costumier, put on a better show last year than we thought at the time.'

# Big Trouble For Ben

Schoolboy Ben enjoyed trying to cut a bit of a dash. And why not? If you aren't in the mood to stamp your individuality on this dreary old world at the age of 16, then you never will be.

Sadly for Ben, the officers of the law at Redland, Bristol, did not share his enthusiasm. They simply could not see that any young gentleman would swagger about with a silver-topped stick just for the sartorial fun of it. They therefore ran him in for carrying an offensive weapon! It took two hours to convince them that Beau Brummell lives.

Ben was justifiably furious about the whole thing. So was his father, who commented somewhat sharply: 'They'll be arresting people for carrying tennis rackets next!'

# Solid Defences

Malcolm Finlayson is now a rich and successful businessman. But life was not always quite so easy.

On November 13, 1948, Finlayson was playing in goal for Third Division Millwall at an away match against Walsall. With his side 1 - 0 up, Finlayson was kicked in the face and had to be taken to a nearby hospital for stitches. Thus repaired and almost as good as new, the goalie returned to the ground.

By this time Millwall were losing 3 - 1 and the gates were firmly shut. Thumping on them did no good at all. He was well and truly locked out.

The unfortunate Finlayson, dazed, in pain, and feeling far from well, was obliged to climb over the fence to get back in, and when he did actually walk on to the field, he was so groggy that he set off for the wrong end.

He did wind up with some satisfaction, however, for his side eventually won 6 – 5.

# Dog Day Afternoon

Stephen Winkworth, compiler of a popular book entitled *Famous Sporting Fiascos*, decided to call on the Voice of Cricket, John Arlott, to glean material for his volume. Mr Arlott, who has sadly now declared his innings closed and retreated to a fastness on the isle of Alderney, was, at the time of Mr Winkworth's visit, engaged upon the obituary of a very dear friend, and did not wish to be interrupted.

Pressing on regardless, the seeker after calamity ventured: 'Like if a dog ran on to the pitch and bit the wicket-keeper. That sort of thing, sort of...'

Arlott glowered at his unwanted visitor from beneath his Healey-style eyebrows and enquired dauntingly, 'Is that funny?'

Soon afterwards, and none the wiser for his trouble, Mr Winkworth went on his way.

The hand of Nemesis, however, never far from the heels of such dogged researchers, then revealed itself in the thoroughly unpleasant guise of a filthy mongrel cur, which scuttled across the road, as the unfortunate Winkworth was leaving the house, and bit him on the lower leg.

# More Than They Could Chiew

When £2,000 worth of limp and soggy noodles were returned by angry customers to the Tai Cheong noodle factory in Lancashire, the bosses looked round furiously for the culprit. They found him in the shape of chief noodle-mixer Van Chiew Tu, who had mistakenly thought that nipping away from his duties for the odd quick smoke or drink would not affect the delicate balance of the recipe handed down from Tai to Tai over generations.

He blundered again when he decided to take his employers to court claiming unfair dismissal. The case was dismissed, leaving him to pay the costs of the proceedings.

Which all just goes to show the truth of the old Chinese saying (all old Chinese say it): Noodle mixer who get it wrong, get chopstick chop and wind up doing pancake roll into street chop chop.

# Insoluble Tablet

A mysterious stone tablet was discovered among a load of prehistoric relics in 1838 by archeologists digging in the Grave Creek Mound in West Virginia.

For nearly a century over 60 linguists puzzled over the hieroglyphic characters engraved on the tablet. Controversy raged. Could it be Runic or Etruscan? Or was it, perhaps, a hitherto unknown ancient language?

There were red faces indeed in these academic circles when, in 1930, a young man endeavouring to get an unusually angled photograph of the now-famous 'mystery relic' discovered their mistake.

Quite decipherable from this perspective, the inscription, which was in English, read:

## BILL STUMP'S STONE
## October 14, 1838

# A Dream Of Freedom

In 1880 Alessandro Saraceni was accused of killing a man whose body was found on the Naples road shortly after Saraceni had passed by on his mule. Saraceni hotly protested his innocence, but to no avail. The jury found him guilty and recommended that, in his case, life imprisonment should mean just that and nothing mamby-pamby like twenty years' hard labour.

So the unfortunate Alessandro languished in prison for thirty-two years. Then, one night, his warders were disturbed to hear the old man screaming in his sleep.

He told his captors he had seen King Victor of Italy on the brink of assassination. The warders informed the prison governor who thought, not unreasonably, that the whole thing was a joke, which he shared with the head of the state police. The police chief was a little more superstitious and was struck by the similarities in the dream to a ride through Rome that King Victor and Queen Elena were to take the following day.

Strange to relate, the next day, as the Royal couple drove through the eternal city, an anarchist named D'Alba fired three shots at the King. But the assassination attempt was foiled because the police were on their guard thanks to poor old Alessandro, still rotting in his cell.

Kings are very busy people and Saraceni spent another fourteen years in prison before Victor heard of the dream that had helped to save his life. The least he could do was to order that the case be reheard, so, in 1926, the old man was finally set free. He had been cleared at last, and in his place the mule was found guilty. Not that it bothered the homicidal animal. It had been dead for years.

★　　★　　★　　★

*. . . . . . . . . . . . . .There is absolutely nothing like a parade to get the average citizen of the United States lit up with excitement. Not, however, on the day in Ventura, California, when a drum major hurled his baton high into the air – where it hit a power cable, melted, blacked out ten blocks, put a radio station off the air and started a grass fire. . . . . . . . . . . . . . . . . . . . . . . . . . . . . . . . . . . . . . . . . . . . . .*

# Seating Plan

Emperor Menelik II of Abyssinia was much impressed with a report of the first electric chair being used for executions in New York in 1890. Thinking this was just the thing to bring his nation sizzling into the modern era, he ordered three of the fearful machines.

When they arrived he was most disappointed, because he simply could not get them to work. The silly man had overlooked the fact that his country had no electricity supply.

However, he was a practical man and converted one of the chairs to become the Imperial Throne.

# Tour De Force

Police at the charming Gloucestershire town of Cheltenham were called in to track down a missing tourist. Stanley Elsis from California had booked into a guest house and then vanished, leaving his two suitcases full of clothes.

The riddle was not answered for two weeks, when Mr Elsis turned up again. Red-faced, he explained that he had got lost journeying round the historic town. He could not remember where he was staying and so decided to carry on with his tour of Britain. His travels took him to visit friends in Wales and Scotland, before he wound up back in Cheltenham.

# Jailbirds

Police near Sheffield learnt the hard way that abiding by the letter of the law can be a mistake. Answering a complaint, they took into custody eight ducks that had been found wandering nearby.

The feathered felons soon began disturbing the peace of the local nick, driving the boys in blue quietly quackers with their constant clamouring for food.

Regretting their initial zeal, the policemen had soon placed at the top of their Most Wanted list the owner of the noisy runaways.

# Bureaucrackers

................. *Errors concerning officialese
and gobbledygook* ..........................................................

# Look And Learn Dept

The Defence Ministry sometimes seems disturbingly simple.
They once sent an order to Ladybird Books, the children's
favourites, for a complete set of books explaining how computers
work.

Messrs Ladybird, puzzled, responded by thanking the MoD
for their offered custom, but begged to point out, most
respectfully, that the target audience for the publication in
question was the miniature boffin of around nine years of age.

The MoD wrote back right away, thanking Ladybird for this
clarification, and confirming the order.

# Gaucho Marks

You certainly can't trust the Argentinians, and we can all sleep
more safely in our beds thanks to the beady-eyed vigilance of
the Foreign Office, with a little help from the US State
Department. The FO boys had words with those responsible for
the heading over an item in the agenda for the United Nations
General Assembly deliberations.

It was down as 'The Question of the Malvinas Islands'.
Fearing a dastardly plot by the frightful Johnny Gaucho, our side
bade the UN go away and retitle the item a little less
controversially.

The final result, pleasing to all sides, was a masterpiece of
diplomatic art. The English version referred to the Falkland
Islands (Malvinas), while the Spanish-speaking contingent had it
as Islas Malvinas (Falklands).

# Rest Assured

The 1959 National Insurance Bill assured those of retiring age:
'For the purpose of this part of the schedule a person over
pensionable age, not being an insured person, shall be treated
as an employed person if he would be an insured person were
he under pensionable age and would be an employed person
were he an insured person.'

So *that* was all right.

*. . . . . . . . . . . . .In 1954 the mayor of the*
*Châteauneuf-du-Pape community in France passed a by-law*
*banning all flying saucers from landing in the area . . . . . . . .*

★     ★     ★     ★

# Baby Talk

Those attending a state-run training course on Civil Defence and Welfare wondered what they were there for when they read in a Section Bulletin on emergency midwifery the following encouraging injunction:

'It should be remembered that childbirth is a normal function and Nature should be allowed to take its course.'

Such advice, it might be thought, rendered redundant the very training scheme it illustrated.

# A Vacancy Has Arisen...

The GCHQ at Cheltenham, the Government's top secret and highly leak-prone intelligence centre, advertised in November 1982 for a Russian linguist.

The ad appeared in *The Guardian* the day after superspy Geoffrey Prime, who used his post as a linguist to further his treacherous aims, was jailed for 35 years.

The centre would neither confirm nor deny that the timing of the ad was coincidental.

# Watership Down And Out

It was more than enough to make Hazel's ears go on the droop when, to celebrate 1982 National Tree Week, Hampshire County Council decided to build wire fences around 1,000 young beech trees on the famous leporine beauty spot of Watership Down.

The object: to keep out rabbits.

# As Easy As ABC

A Ministry of Defence publication informed an avidly waiting world:

'In reference A, the cover letter at Reference B is an error. The additions at Annex B to Reference B are already incorporated in Annex A to Reference B, and are those additional items per pack that will be required if the complete schedule at Annex A to Reference B are approved.'

Let us all hope with every fibre of our being that they never are.

# Eightpenny Dreadful

After fourteen years working in a laundry and a further fourteen as a café waitress, Mrs Rosa Curran joined her husband in running a Whitbread pub in South London.

At the age of sixty-five, Mrs Curran decided it was time to call it a day, and was looking forward to a comfortable and problem-free retirement.

She was understandably concerned, and later furious, when the Department of Health and Social Security informed her that, after fifty years of paying stamps, she was entitled to a pension of – 8p a week!

A DHSS spokesman said: 'The 8p is based on contributions Mrs Curran paid to the graduated pension scheme between 1961 and 1975!'

The Currans must now live on a brewery – rather than a Beveridge – pension.

# Don't Leave The Lab Without It

The credit card organization that is so anxious to ensure that you do not leave home without its passport to plastic happiness safely in your pocket issued a 'personal invitation' to Mr C. Cell, Mutation Unit, University of Sussex.

And it certainly did nicely as a source of hilarity for the team comprising the *MRC Cell Unit* at the university!

# War And (At Last) Peace 1

The Pyrenean mini-state of Andorra is perhaps best known as an excellent spot for tourists to stop off for a carload of duty free goods on the way home from sunny Spain. However, it also has a war record second to none.

Because of an oversight, the Versailles Peace Treaty which ended the Great War of 1914-18 failed to include Andorra. So, in 1939, with the Second World War well under way, the tiny principality discovered to its horror that officially it was still fighting the first.

A quick and private treaty with Germany concluded hostilities.

# Cross Bar

Councillors of the City of Oxford had hardly had time to pat themselves on the back for their conservationist and environmentally-conscious introduction of five miles of cycle-ways when they were brought up short by an accusation from furious feminists. It seems that the road signs showed only a man's bike with a crossbar – grossly sexist in anyone's highway code!

The prospect of Women's Rights demonstrations in the city of gleaming spires was too much for the councillors, who promised that in future all signs would show both a man's and a woman's bike.

# Shell Shockers

Those wonderful eggheads at the Min. of Ag. Fish and Food Centre for Avian Epidemiology, (which those intelligent enough to be reading this book will not need to be told means the study of sick birds) down at Gloucester, got themselves into a rare old flap.

They were called out one day to a battery farm to crack the riddle of some erratic layers. The hens in the middle and upper tiers of the battery were not laying as many eggs as those on the ground floor.

What a puzzler! Could those on the two upper levels be coming down with some dreadful ague? The experts (I resist the temptation to call them eggsperts) at first suspected inadequate ventilation, and then vaccination problems, and still later infectious bronchitis. Heads were scratched late into the night.

The answer, when it came, was dazzlingly simple. A former employee of the battery had been stealing the eggs, and had left the bottom tier alone because he had a bad back.

★　★　★　★

. . . . . . . . . . . . . . . *United States President McKinley was assured by the Director of the US Patent Office in 1899 that 'everything that can be invented has been invented'* . . . . . . . .

★　★　★　★

# Weather, Or Not

A Governmental committee asked the Meteorological Office in Bracknell for a definitive ruling on when winter begins and ends. The Met waded in with an immediate answer: 'Winter begins when all the leaves have fallen off the trees,' they said, adding the further scientific ruling: 'And it ends when the bulbs start coming up again.'

No doubt the Governmental committee presented them with a very cold front and a severe touch of frost.

# Turned Over By A New Leaf

Pensioners Sid and Sarah Coulson, and all their neighbours, were delighted when the thoughtful Sheffield City Council planted 11 lime trees along their road at Greenland Close, in Darnall.

But six years later they had changed their minds, for the trees had spread their roots, as trees are wont to do, and turned the Coulsons' home into a crumbling ruin. The council had to rehouse the couple while structural repairs were carried out.

They also gave the too vigorous trees the chop.

# World Weary

The lugubrious-sounding and forward-looking End of the World Society decided to go down in style with a Doomsday Party at Bude in Cornwall. They called it all off, however, when local magistrates refused to grant a special late-night drinks licence.

Apparently the local beaks felt that the end of the world was not a special event.

★　★　★　★

*..............Jean Cocteau's 1956 film* **The Seashell and the Clergyman** *was banned by the vigilant British Board of Film Censors because 'the film is apparently meaningless, but if it has any meaning it is doubtless objectionable'......*

# There Were These Tree Fellers

Mr Hew Watt of the Nature Conservancy Council amazed, nay stunned, his audience at a seminar at University College, London, when he told them that he had grown weary of small boys with foul mouths intruding into his garden in order to steal conkers – so weary that he had chopped down his trio of venerable chestnut trees.

# A Lot Of Awful Honesty In Brazil

Joao Damico, who proclaimed himself to be the most successful car thief in Brazil, was also destined to wind up as the most disgruntled. Interviewed after his ultimate arrest, he snarled: 'I do not understand the world any more. I have been a car thief for 25 years and this is the first time police officers have failed to accept a bribe. I am seriously disappointed by this unpatriotic behaviour.'

Senhor Damico went on to describe his local sheriff as 'a monster of honesty.'

# Extended Credit

James Grant died on 29 June. His son Ronald was surprised, therefore, on opening his late father's credit card account some two and a half weeks later, to notice a debit of £7.56 paid to Travellers Fare Restaurant on 8 July. In a letter to the company concerned, Ronald enquired interestedly:

'I did not realize that such facilities were available, or indeed necessary, on the journey my father has just undertaken, nor indeed that the trip lasted so long. Do let me know for what period of time your credit facilities are extended in these circumstances.'

In their letter of apology, the company wisely declined to respond to the latter remarks.

★　　★　　★　　★

*.............For those of you who have not heard, here is a news flash from the Compleat Works of the Department of Technical Co-operation Departmental Fire Precautions and Instructions: 'Most fires are caused by some igniting source coming into contact with combustible material'*.............................

★　　★　　★　　★

# Tube Boob

London Transport may pride themselves on the many and varied souvenirs and information leaflets they produce for tourists. Advertisements for T-shirts, country walk guides and the recently opened LT Museum emblazon every double-decker and tube escalator in the metropolis. However, a poster on display at London Bridge underground station cannot rank among the Information Office's most successful efforts. Advising travellers on how to get to any of the main line British Rail stations, the instructions for each possible route tell passengers to start off on the District or Piccadilly line. All well and good, you may think. But London Bridge is on the Northern line.

# Safety Last

In furtherance of their campaign for safer toys, the United States Consumer Product Safety Commission had 80,000 fun badges made ready for distribution to the nation's kids.

Sadly, they had to junk the lot. The badges had sharp edges and pins that came undone with distressing and painful ease. And they were brightly coloured in lead paint.

# No Mercy For The Angels

Student nurses at a West Country hospital received letters from their bosses offering them congratulations on passing their exams. The letters then went on to tell them that they were fired. Hospital administrators explained to the girls that they were being made redundant because there were no permanent jobs to offer them. However, if they had *failed* to pass their exams they could have stayed for another six months, while they studied for retakes.

The chief administrator said: 'We make it perfectly clear that we can't guarantee jobs.' But one of the student nurses was totally unimpressed by this argument. She said: 'I can't help feeling that we are being used as cheap labour.'

# Danger! Woman Driver Behind

There are those who think that it is *always* a mistake to allow a woman behind the wheel of a car. In Memphis, Tennessee it *certainly* would be – you could get arrested for it. According to an old by-law, a female must not drive an automobile – unless she is preceded down the street by a man carrying a red flag!

★    ★    ★    ★

. . . . . . . . . . . . . . *Frenchman Paul Hubert was 21 years into a life sentence when, in 1884, his case was reopened because bungling bureaucrats realized that he had been convicted of murdering himself!* . . . . . . . . . . . . . . . . . . . . . . . . . . . . . . .

# They Must Be Inthane!

The Department of Education and Science was running a bizarre risk when it decided to close the Roman Catholic Newman College of Education. Not to put too fine a point upon it, the DES mandarins might have expected a rather nasty visitation from well beyond the grave.

The ghost involved would almost certainly have been none other than Wulfwine, an 11th century Saxon lord who owned the land on which the college stands. He decided that no one but the Catholic Church should use the land for all time on pain of a fearful curse. And Wulfwine seems to have been a dab, if bloody, hand at making sure the curse stuck.

When the Protestant Dudley family took over the land, they became spectacular victims. The hated Edmund Dudley was beheaded by Henry VIII, and his son, the Duke of Northumberland, went the same way attempting to put Lady Jane Grey on the throne.

Lady Jane and her husband, yet another Dudley, also lost their heads in the plot. Robert Dudley, Earl of Leicester, died of the fever while failing to lead an Elizabethan force to victory in the Netherlands.

Since these facts came to light, the Education Department, recognizing that discretion is the better part, has reversed its decision, the college land has been returned to Mother Church and peace reigns in Wulfwine's domain.

# A Six Day Week Shalt Thou Labour

The canny framers of by-laws at Thurston County, Washington, certainly knew the time of day, if not the day of the week, when they were trying to avoid paying police and firemen overtime for Sunday working. The citizens of the County opened their local weekly newspaper one Sunday morning and couldn't believe their eyes. Although the date was correct enough, the paper proclaimed it to be *Monday*.

The explanation was simple enough: the powers-that-be had simply decided that Sunday was abolished.

# Stone Blind

The City Corporation planning department really blew their cool when photographs of London's tallest tower block, the Nat West Building, landed on their busy desks. They never granted permission for those statues perched on the top storey, they expostulated. Then some sharper-eyed character pointed out that the figures in the snap weren't statues at all, but workmen!

# ...What The Left Hand Was Doing

During Prohibition (1920-33) in the United States the sale, manufacture and transportation of alcoholic beverages was rendered illegal by the 18th Amendment to the Constitution.

Somehow or other, however, nobody ever got round to informing the bureaucrats at the US Department of Agriculture of this. So, throughout the entire thirteen year 'dry' period, they continued to distribute leaflets detailing ways of extracting alcohol from apples, bananas, pumpkins, etc. It could only have happened in America – land of the Free and Speakeasy!

# Video Fun And Games

When the Inland Revenue Staff Federation decided to produce a video cassette explaining to their members how the new technology might affect their future, the Inland Revenue Board (representing the employers' side) stepped in. They announced that the cassette could not be shown on government property (i.e. the 50 VHS video recorders specifically hired for the purpose) unless a video of Sir Lawrence Airey, the Board's chief, were played immediately after, putting an official reply.

The Staff Federation agreed readily enough, but when 50 video cassettes duly arrived from the Board, they were found to be totally unplayable.

Due to some 'unfortunate' bureaucratic blunder, Sir Lawrence's reply had been recorded on to Betamax cassettes, which cannot be used on the VHS machines. Talk about 'incompatibility'!

# Trial By Duel

Sometimes, as we all know, the law is an ass. Such a case certainly occurred in 1817 when a certain Mr Ashford witnessed the murder of his sister by a man named Thornton.

The guilty man immediately challenged Ashford to decide the case by armed combat and appeared at the appointed time in full battle regalia, complete with a lance and a sword.

Not surprisingly, Ashford failed to turn up for the duel. He was busy with his lawyers preparing the case against Thornton. But

When he came before the court, however, the murderer claimed that he had already won the case by default.

The judge was forced to admit he was right. Parliament had foolishly neglected ever to abolish the medieval custom of trial by one-to-one combat.

Needless to say, the situation was at once rectified so that no such miscarriage of justice could occur again, but Thornton remained free.

Under English law, no man can be 'tried' for the same crime twice.

# No Need To Worry

The spirit of the men who carry the mail seems to be unquenchable, and it spans the globe. At a recent House of Representatives hearing in Washington, Mr Ralph H. Jusell, the postal services civil defence co-ordinator, assured bemused Congressmen that a mere nuclear holocaust would not stop the mail getting through. He insisted: 'Those that are left will get their mail.'

Under the plan, drawn up in 1981, express, registered and other special delivery services might have to be suspended, for the time being at least. But first class letters would still get top priority.

Indeed, the optimistic Mr Jusell was able to go further, proving that those faceless legions who run public enterprise really do have an appreciation of the difficulties faced by the ordinary folk at times of inconvenience, such as during World War Three. The mail will still be delivered even if the survivors run out of stamps.

★　　★　　★　　★

...............*The census conducted in 1981 by the Australian Bureau of Statistics showed 3,287,035 men saying they were married. On the other hand, only 3,264,179 women declared themselves to be wed. Police are now looking for 22,856 missing wives!*........................

★　　★　　★　　★

# Right On The Button

A new pressure group calling itself Lawyers v the Bomb has come up with the heartening news that, in the event of a nuclear holocaust, we may all have a very good case for legal action against those responsible. Their launch press release stated categorically that 'the use of nuclear weapons would be a clear breach of international law', while offering the opinion that 'the manufacture and deployment of these weapons may well also be a crime punishable in a court of international law.'

So now we all know what to do in that four minutes before the bomb drops – phone our lawyers!

# Joint Board Bard

During 1982 a circular was issued by the Joint Matriculation Board Examinations Council. It declared that, because of a marked increase in 'the incidence of rubric infringements by Candidates', it had been decided to modify the format of the English Literature (Advanced) Paper I. In future, in order to avoid any possibility of confusion, section B will consist of essay questions on the plays of someone called Shakespaere.

No, this is not a recently discovered master writer of untold literary merit, but simply an 'infringement' of the accepted rules of spelling.

# Defence Defect

When a British national newspaper published the tonnage of the Royal Navy's proposed new diesel-electric submarine, a flustered Ministry of Defence Press Attaché accused their Naval Correspondent of betraying an official secret.

Astonished, the journalist protested: 'There must be some mistake. It was you who gave me those figures.'

'Correction,' came the mind-boggling reply. 'We gave you the information calculated in metric tonnes – which is not secret.'

It would seem that the MoD fondly believes that the Russians do not possess such pillars of Western civilization as the conversion table or the pocket calculator – the necessary wherewithal for extracting the real tonnage from the elaborate coding of metric tonnes! It certainly makes you think...

# Little Blacked Book

In 1930 a court in Boston, Massachusetts banned Theodore Dreiser's novel of murder and adultery among New York industrialists, *An American Tragedy* (1925), as 'an insult to a civilized society'.

Tough luck on students across the Charles River at Harvard University, where the book, regarded to this day both as a pillar of twentieth century American literature and an important sociological document, was required reading for some courses.

# War And (At Last) Peace 2

1966 was a big year in the turbulent history of the charming border town of Berwick-on-Tweed, for it was only then that the town's 110 years of war with Russia came to an end.

Although the Crimean War was concluded in 1856, an oversight in the Paris Peace Treaty excluded Berwick (traditionally referred to separately in State documents) from this outbreak of non-aggression. Then, at last, in 1966 a Soviet Government envoy made a good will visit to the town and peace broke out under an official seal.

As the Mayor of Berwick put it: 'Now the Russians can sleep peacefully in their beds.'

# Chequeing Out

Gerhard Koenig of Munich was not a frequent visitor to his bank. In fact, the officials of the branch with whom he had his account were a little puzzled that the only time their services were called into action was when his State pension cheques were paid in. It took the alert bank staff 7 whole years to realize that perhaps all was not as it should be.

Finally, they reported the inactivity to the authorities, who called at Herr Koenig's flat. They found nothing but a skeleton. The old gentleman had died – some seven years earlier.

# Giro In A Spin

Definitely overworked and probably underpaid, the hard-pressed boys and girls at the social security office in Exeter, Devon, simply stopped answering the phones in the afternoons, because they were so far behind in their labours.

They knew that most of the calls were from people complaining that their Giro cheques were late, that lateness in turn being caused by the backlog.

A bewildered official said: 'If we answer the phone and then have to check out the queries, we'll just get even further behind.'

# Board Stiff

July 29, 1966, was a red letter day for the Board of Trade Journal. True to its departmental terms of reference, it was splendidly international in correcting a previous entry:

> **In the list of films registered during the week ended 15 July, 1966, the title of the film *DeGaulle Stone Operation* should read *The Great DeGaulle Stone Operation* and the title of the film *The Great Napoleon Blownaparte* should read *Napoleon Blownaparte*.**

Book now to avoid disappointment.

# Yet More Hot News

The Civil Service is most concerned to protect its officers in the event of an igniting source getting anywhere near combustible material.

Hence this Minute (Civil Servicese for Memo) on the subject of fire precautions: 'Fire practice. This was discussed with the Fire Prevention Officer quite recently and the main objections were:

(1) that if the alarm bell rang, the occupants might think there was a fire and injuries could be caused among the old and infirm staff in trying to evacuate the building; and

(2) if regular fire practices were held, the staff would in time treat it as a joke and not in a serious manner.

There is more, but I feel the world is not yet ready to face it.

# You Said It

*............... Errors concerning
the spoken and written word ...........................................*

# Snow Business Like Car Business

'I just pray to God that the UK Government spend their North Sea oil revenue intelligently, instead of continuing to pour money into subsidizing businesses that are losers from day one.'

The speaker, during a frank, free and fearless BBC Radio 4 interview on July 15, 1979, was John Z. De Lorean.

★　　★　　★　　★

*.............A woman walked into her local bookshop and asked the bewildered assistant: 'Have you got Thomas Hardy's* Tess of the Dormobiles?'*.....................*

★　　★　　★　　★

*...............The Rules of Entry for the Miss Nude USA Competition included the stipulation that contestants must betray 'taste in clothing'.......................*

★　　★　　★　　★

# Deaf Ears

Lord Kelvin, President of the Royal Society, came to the following conclusion in 1894: 'Radio has no future.' At around the same time he also declared: 'Heavier-than-air flying machines are impossible.'

# Time And Tim

1965 was not a particularly good year for Timothy Leary, the high priest of America's drug culture...but it was certainly a better one than 1980.

In 1965 he predicted the collapse of the United States within 15 years. When the deadline passed without too many signs of a wobble, much less a total collapse, he shrugged off queries by saying: 'What is time, my dears? You are talking to the man who brought you the 1960s.'

# Request Bequest

The pressures of non-stop record-playing and compering can become too much for the average mortal. One disc-jockey certainly found it so as he announced on a request programme:

'This is for Mrs Brenda Jones who is one hundred years old today. But I'm told she's dead with-it.'

# Shock Exclusive

In 1978 a British National newspaper stunned its readers with the headline:

## ...POPE DIES AGAIN...

★　　★　　★　　★

*. . . . . . . . . . . . .Following the horrific financial disaster of his movie Raise The Titanic, Lord Grade was heard to remark of his mistaken venture: 'It would have been cheaper to lower the Atlantic'. . . . . . . . . . . . . . . . . . . . . . . . . . . . . . . . . . . . . . . . . . . . . . . . .*

★　　★　　★　　★

# A Tight Hand On The Reins

Advanced advertising material for a club's gala night contained the memorably phrased promise:

*The evening will conclude with a toast to the incoming president in champagne kindly supplied by the outgoing president, drunk as usual at midnight.*

No doubt there was soon an outgoing Press Secretary as well!

# Doctor Death

A Paris newspaper once ran two unrelated paragraphs together to form the following howler:

'Dr F. has been appointed to the position of head physician to the Hôpital de la Charité. Orders have been issued to the authorities for the immediate extension of the cemetery at Montparnasse.'

# Roads To Ruin

Several leading motor manufacturers have lost something (usually sales) in the translation of their car model names into foreign languages.

Ford have had considerable experience of this. They planned to introduce a glamorous new model in Mexico and eventually came up with the name Caliente. They were, however, obliged to have a rethink and call the car the S22 instead, for in Mexican-Spanish *caliente* is a slang word for street-walker. The company had yet another fearful disappointment when they discovered that Cortina in Japanese translates as the highly undesirable and unmarketable 'broken down old car'.

General Motors is another giant company which had its problems down Mexico way. They launched their Chevrolet Nova to a crescendo of hilarity: in Spanish, no-va means 'won't go'.

The Triumph Acclaim had to be renamed for the German market because the best translation available was the totally unacceptable 'Zieg Heil'.

However, first prize must go to the world's number one motor manufacturer, Rolls Royce, who did not realize that in Germany (East or West) Silver Mist meant nothing other than what one might tastefully describe as 'human waste'.

# Bishop's Move

The Rt Rev. Timothy Dudley-Smith is Bishop of Thetford. He also became well known as the contributor of 46 of the new *Hymns For Today's Church*, which did not find universal approval among the faithful.

However, the Bishop caused even more scratching of heads when he announced: 'I'm tone deaf and cannot sing a note.'

★　　★　　★　　★

. . . . . . . . . . . . . *A scathing three-word judgment was all that was vouchsafed to Hollywood heart-throb Clark Gable after his first screen test: 'Ears too big.' The author of the remark has wisely preserved his anonymity. . . . . . . . . . . . . . . . . . . . . . .*

★　　★　　★　　★

# Anything Could Happen

The effect was shattering for the big-selling vodka firm whose advertisement declared:

*'I THOUGHT THE KARMA SUTRA WAS AN INDIAN RESTAURANT UNTIL I DISCOVERED SMIRNOFF.'*

An executive, explaining why this particular ad was dropped from the campaign, said: 'We conducted a survey and discovered that 60 per cent of the people *did* think it was an Indian restaurant.'

★　　★　　★　　★

. . . . . . . . . . . . . *In 1948 Warren Austin, the well-meaning but bungling United States Ambassador to the United Nations, implored the warring Arabs and Jews to behave 'like good Christians'. . . . . . . . . . . . . . . . . . . . . . . . . . . . . . . . . . . . . .*

# Success On El Plato

Many Britons are, quite rightly, still dubious about foreign food, in spite of the proliferation of Indian, Chinese, Italian and other ethnic restaurants in this country. To many British eyes, not to mention stomachs, there is something especially ominous about what you get when you go abroad. (It is obviously all part of an extremely nasty plot to stop us taking over the Common Market.)

Conscious of the gastronomic culture gap, many helpful restaurateurs in the holiday hotspots now knock out a multi-lingual menu.

Unfortunately, the proprietor of one such eating house at Moraira, on Spain's sun-drenched (as they say) Costa Dorada, may have his heart in the right place, but his English phrasebook has clearly been left to languish in his other suit. Visitors to this palace of culinary delight will be presented with the following:

---

## MENU

Aside Rice Ham Fish
Crumbled Eggs with Tomato


Goose Barnacles
Natural Fish Knife (piece)
Gordon Blu
Thigh Lambskin


Pineapple Wirsch
Special Ice from The House
Frost Pie

---

And to follow? Presumably, rampant indigestion!

# Head's Roll

An advertisement for the headship of a junior school in London's East End appeared in the *Times Educational Supplement*. It revealed the following apparently contradictory information:

   'The roll is largely Muslim. Strong Church of England links and a regular communicant preferred.'

★   ★   ★   ★

.............*In 1959 the head of the International Monetary Fund announced that world inflation was over*.....................................................

★   ★   ★   ★

# Dear Me

The *Chingford Classified*, surely one of the great news organs of our time, printed this sublime description of the Queen Elizabeth I Hunting Lodge in Epping Forest:

> **It now stands mute, but if you stand still, eyes closed, willing the 20th century to roll back, can you hear the ghostly notes of an English hunting horn? Or the last swish of a Victorian petticoat? Can you catch an echo of its shrill, carousing, dog-baying heyday? When the open galleries on the top floors...echoed with the oaths...of noisy hunting fans. Where in later years, too worn to ride, the Queen and her favourites waited for dear after dear to come within bolt range of their crossbows.**

# The Word Of The Lord

A newly-revised edition of the Bible, which went on sale in 1982, almost appeared with a printing error which would have been a disastrous benediction for the idle among our number.

As I am sure you do not need reminding, Exodus 20, verse 9 should read: 'Six days you shall labour and do all your work.' However, in the new version it actually appeared as: 'Six days you should not work.'

Happily, this somewhat crucial error was picked up while the Bible was in proof form. A spokesman for publishers Samuel Bagster said: 'It would have been a disaster.'

# Taxing Problems

John Maynard Keynes, the famous economist, took time off from diagnosing the problems of the modern world to offer the following philosophical observations:

'The avoidance of taxes is the only intellectual pursuit that still carries any reward.'

# Alas Poor Schnozzle

John Barrymore, an occasional drinking companion of the great Jimmy 'Schnozzle' Durante, once told the melancholy man with the big nose: 'You should play Hamlet.'

Durante shook his head. 'To hell with them small towns,' he said. 'I'll stick to New York.'

★ ★ ★ ★

*.............During the hard-fought and exciting 1949 Oxford and Cambridge University Boat Race, BBC commentator John Snagge got so carried away by the excitement that he heard himself say: 'I don't know who's ahead. It's either Oxford or Cambridge'.................*

★ ★ ★ ★

# Popsuey

Back in the halcyon days of the 1970s, when the spirit of good will was abroad in the air between the United States and the People's Republic of China, the new accord was celebrated with (what else?) supplies of Pepsi Cola to the yellow hordes.

The slogan 'Come alive with Pepsi' had been a great success in the West and seemed ideally full of Eastern promise too. So the company's ad men had it translated into Mandarin – or at least that was their intention.

Sadly, they were obliged to make a rapid return to the drawing board because the best translation that could be achieved was: 'Pepsi brings your ancestors back from the grave.'

Lipsmackinthirstquenchingraverobbin...

# Gun Law

A woman was committed under the Mental Health Act for shooting her husband with a .410 shotgun. After the judge had pronounced his decision, the prosecution – not unreasonably – asked that the gun be destroyed. The judge disagreed, declaring such an act both wasteful and unnecessary. He may have had a point, but his final suggestion must surely go down as a grossly insensitive blunder. Describing the weapon as 'a nice little folding .410', he went on: 'I think it should go to the son. It should give him a great deal of pleasure.' The mind boggles!

# Fowl Play

Finger-lickin' good, but head-scratchin' puzzlin' was the sign which hung in pride of place in the window of a South of England Kentucky Fried Chicken dispensary.

It boasted:

**OPEN SEVEN DAYS A WEEK, EXCLUDING SUNDAYS**

# What A Loo!

Those responsible for the placing of an official notice in the litter-strewn Ladies Room at London's National Film Theatre must surely have been mistaken – or *has* yet another of London's bridges found its way across the Atlantic? The notice read:

*WE APOLOGIZE TO VISITORS FOR THE DETERIORATION IN THIS TOILET AREA. THIS WAS CAUSED BY MOVEMENT OF WATERLOO BRIDGE.*

# Traffic Copped

The man from the Automobile Association who delights listeners to the London Broadcasting Company with descriptions of the misery they are going to face if they attempt to get to work in their cars, surpassed himself one merry morn.

He told the waiting millions: 'Traffic is very heavy at the moment, so if you are thinking of leaving now, you'd better set off a few minutes earlier.'

Do not adjust your trannies, there is a fault in the man from the AA.

# Pieces Of Fate

.................. *Errors concerning*
*unavoidable misfortune* .................................................

# Pastor Master

The Rev. James Boysell, hard-hitting pastor of a church in New Jersey, was a man who knew what to look for – and between which lines to read. When his car ran out of petrol in heavy traffic, he was suspicious. When the church chimes went out of order and the church central heating furnace exploded, he was suspicious and alarmed. When he entered the church one day and a board fell on his head, he was suspicious, alarmed and absolutely certain: it was the work of the Devil, Satan himself.

At the end of that demonic week in 1940 he startled parishioners with a pulpit denunciation of the Devil and all his sulphurous works. To assist the spirit of the meeting Rev. Boysell had engaged the services of a young man, who stood before him clad in Satanic costume. The pastor berated him with logic and ordered him to be gone. As a grand finale to the symbolic ceremony, the pastor then chased the 'Devil' down the aisle and out of the door.

Whereupon Rev. Boysell fell over and broke his arm.

# Suspended Sentence

It is not customary to find much light-heartedness in the air on a hanging morn, but on February 23, 1885 at least one man managed to walk away from the execution shed with a decided spring in his step. The condemned man was 19-year-old John Lee who had been due to pay the supreme penalty at Exeter Prison. The thoughtful authorities had erected a brand new gallows for the occasion. Lee, hooded and manacled, stood on the trap awaiting the drop into eternity. And waited and waited, for the trap stubbornly refused to open.

The killer was taken back to his cell while engineers inspected the offending mechanism. The executioner had a test pull of the lever and the trap sprung open with awesome efficiency. Lee was brought back with due apologies for this unseemly hanging about. Again the trap refused to open. Again the wretched Lee was returned to his cell.

The process was repeated once more, with the same result, before the authorities decided to call the whole thing off and commute the sentence to life imprisonment.

# Wrong Arm Of The Law

Police Constable Frank Melia called at an address in a run down area of Liverpool. The smell of the hovel was matched only by the scruffy appearance of the mother, father and five children who lived there. Melia, a fastidious man, politely and sensibly declined a cup of tea and perched uncomfortably on the edge of the greasy sofa. As he prepared to pursue his inquiries, he saw out of the corner of his eye a furry creature of verminous mien which was crawling up the arm of the sofa.

The constable knew a rat when he saw one and, with reactions as sharp as the creases in his trousers, whipped out his truncheon and walloped the tiny creature into eternity. The family gazed in silence for a moment before one of the urchins responded to Melia's triumphant glow with the words: 'Hey, Mister, why d'you kill my gerbil?'

★　　★　　★　　★

*.............American golfer Elaine Johnson certainly started a bit of a storm in a B-cup when a shot hit a tree and landed in her bra. She told tournament officials: 'I don't mind taking a two-stroke penalty, but I'm damned if I'm going to play the ball where it lies.'......................*

★　　★　　★　　★

# Right Up And Away

Moira Haggerton wanted to keep her 9-year-old son amused while she was out shopping. What better than a video of one of the blockbuster *Superman* movies?

But when Moira returned to her house at Grindon, Sunderland, she could hardly believe her eyes. Her aim had been more than achieved, for there was the lad sitting still, enrapt, goggling at the TV screen. On which was showing an incredibly naughty porn movie.

The manager of the video hire shop admitted that his face was red over the blue movie. 'It was a slip-up,' he said. 'My assistant didn't check the tape before it went out.'

# This Is A Stick-Down

A Scandinavian bank-robber who failed to check the efficiency of his shotgun paid the penalty for his carelessness when he tried to pull off a big haul in a city bank. On whipping the gun from under his raincoat with the familiar cry 'Don't move! This is a stick-up', he was appalled to see the barrel pointing innocuously at the floor. After several vain attempts to snap the barrel into its correct ready-for-action position, the robber threw the useless weapon to the floor with a disgusted 'Oh, forget it', and rushed out of the building!

# Rail Fare À La Française

It is claimed that many a culinary creation has been born out of mishap and disaster. This is certainly true of the much-heralded French vegetable dish known as *pommes soufflées*.

A nineteenth century French chef was hired to prepare a celebratory banquet to mark the opening of a new railway line. As he was preparing the meal at one of the new stations, a message reached the *maître de cuisine* that the trainload of dignitaries would be delayed. Accordingly, he removed his half-cooked *pommes frites* from the oil and began philosophically to prepare a new batch.

Then he was told that there had been a mistake and that the train was even now pulling into the station, on time after all. In desperation, the chef plunged the half-cooked potatoes back into the oil and watched with amazement as they turned from soggy and unappetizing-looking lumps into puffy brown crisp ovals.

Later, on being congratulated on this culinary delight, the chef merely commented with typical Gallic *sang froid*; 'But, messieurs, they were only *pommes soufflées*.'

★　★　★　★

............*Robbers who held up a lorry at Lenham, in Kent, fled in empty-handed disgust when they discovered the cargo they were attempting to hijack was nothing more exciting than dog food and toilet rolls*..................

# Prince Of Bails

Frederick Louis, Prince of Wales and eldest son of George II, was the first royal to take a big interest in cricket. In the end he was quite carried away by the game.

Having caught the cricket bug, an affliction impossible to cure, while watching Surrey playing their dreaded rivals from Middlesex in 1733, he went on to captain Surrey and London only four years later. When he died in 1751, his death was attributed to a painful blow in the side – from a cricket ball.

# Home and dry

A thief who was surprised by the returning owner as he attempted to break into a house in Carlisle, hid his identity by swathing himself in the wet washing which hung on the line in the garden. He then coolly proceeded to a neighbouring house, broke in and stole a spin drier. He got clean away.

# Fishy Tale

Peter Fowler and his pal, Dennis Guest, became two anglers in a tangle when they were marooned on an island in the middle of a fast-flowing river. They used a ladder as a bridge in the River Trent at Torksey, but some other helpful anglers on the bank unwittingly took it with them when they knocked off after an enjoyable day's sport. Resourceful Dennis managed to climb up a rope to the top of a railway bridge, one of whose supports stood on the island. But Peter, who was a beefy 20 stones, was nothing like so lucky. The rope snapped as he tried to haul himself up. Dennis set off to find help, and four hours later the fire brigade turned up and managed to land their cold, wet and hungry catch.

LAUREL
AND
HARDY
RULE
O.K.

# Not His Day

Joe Ramirez, aged 19, jumped into his car and drove to the New York courthouse where he was due to face a traffic charge. By the time his case was called, he realized that his parking meter was about to run out. However, the judge was a reasonable man and he allowed Joe to nip out to insert another coin or two.

At this point events began to take a surreal turn for the unfortunate Joe. As he tried to dash across the street, a policeman collared him and gave him a long lecture on the anti-social nature of jay-walking. He also gave him a ticket. When Joe finally got back to the car, he found that a highly-punctual traffic warden had already slapped on a parking ticket. The somewhat deflated young man went back to court, only to find that the judge had gone for lunch, leaving Joe to feed the meter until the court was ready to sit again.

When the case was heard, Joe was fined $5, but when he pulled out his wallet, he discovered that, what with jay-walking fines and feeding the meter, he had only $2 left. The court clerk agreed to accept the money on condition that the rest of the fine would be paid without delay. Joe went home and was only too pleased to be back behind his own front door, until he found a letter waiting on the mat. To complete a truly wonderful day, it told him: 'Please report for induction in the United States Army.'

★　　★　　★　　★

*.............A course in public speaking at a Leeds adult education centre was given by...Mr A. Stammers..........*

★　　★　　★　　★

# Canny Tale

Little-known Eastern proverb: it is a mistake to let your work take over your life – it can be dangerous.

Failing to heed this warning, a certain Mr Tin, aptly named Thai representative of the Pepsi Cola Company, paid the ultimate penalty when he was shot and killed during a business altercation by a Mr Thongyu Mauksuk of the rival Coca Cola firm. Well, they *said* things go better with Coke!

# Sweet Smell Of Success On The Pavement

Monsieur Coty made millions as the founder of the famous perfume company, but he owed his great success to a lucky break on the pavements of Paris.

As a young man he was obliged to hawk his scents around the stores and one day he took a bottle of a new compound to the manager of a big *magasin*. The manager, smug and dismissive in black coat and striped trousers, rejected the young perfumier's sales pitch and personally showed him the front door.

As the dejected Coty left, he accidentally dropped the bottle and watch dismayed as the contents spread across the pavement. Another effort going down the drain. *Zut alors*! and all that sort of thing.

But then, as in all the best fairy tales, an extraordinary thing happened.

Several well-heeled and exquisitely-scented women customers gathered round and exclaimed: 'My, what a delicious scent,' and, 'Where can we get a bottle, or two?'

The manager did not bat an eyelid as he told the assembled Mesdames: 'Monsieur Coty has been showing me our new, exclusive mixture. We are expecting a large supply by the end of the week.'

Coty took the hint, and an order worth £3,000, and trotted off up the ladder to success.

# Trunk Call

A visitor to Dudley Zoo in the West Midlands got an expensive surprise when she leaned over the barrier to give Flossie the elephant a pat on the head. The elephant was not in the least bit interested in gestures of friendship. A little snack was more in her mind.

Flossie reached out with her trunk, grabbed the woman's handbag, placed it decorously in her mouth, chomped it for the recommended dozen or so times and swallowed it – cash, chequebook, silver pendant and all. This impromptu nibble between meals cost the zoo £30 in compensation.

# Crowning Glory

Edward VII waited a long time to be crowned King, and when he finally got as far as Westminster Abbey for his coronation in 1902, fiasco nearly ruined his big day.

The Archbishop of Canterbury was aged and infirm. He was handed the Imperial Crown by the Dean of Westminster, who was equally feeble. Onlookers feared that the Primate might drop the crown, for it shook in his hands as he held it over the King's head; but he got it on – somehow.

The Keeper of the Muniments and Sub-Librarian of the Abbey revealed later that there had in fact been a fairly glaring error: 'As a matter of fact, the crown was on back to front.'

In the overwhelming euphoria of relief that a total disaster had been averted, no-one appeared to notice the blunder.

'Everyone was so thankful that it was actually on.'

# Cutting Up Rough

The *Gateshead Post*, famed for its fearless reporting of the truth, revealed that a local health centre had put toughened glass in its windows in an attempt to defeat the destructive pleasures of vandals.

Soon afterwards a mother complained to the amazed staff at the centre that her son's head had been cut when a brick he had hurled at the newly-strengthened windows bounced back and hit him.

# How the Wrecktor Fell from Grace

Rector Max Williams turned into a wrecker when he took his car into a garage for a simple oil change.

The havoc got smartly under way when Rev. Williams trundled his Austin automatic into the garage at Newmarket, not far from the Suffolk village of Chevely, where he ministers to pastoral needs. Then his foot simply slipped from brake to accelerator, the car was transmogrified from harmless little runaround into snarling demon, as it fairly roared through the workshop.

Mechanics leaped for safety as the car hit a six-foot ramp, sending the car on top plunging to the ground, its horrified owner still sitting inside, no doubt giving up a quick prayer. Mighty Max then crashed into another car and hammered it into the wall. His own car finally slid gently to a halt, conveniently alongside a workbench.

The rector was unhurt in all but pride, but one mechanic and a customer needed the services of a doctor. The man in the stores was treated for shock.

The garage owner found it difficult to say anything that was not wholly blasphemous, while Mr Williams simply kept repeating to anyone who was capable of listening: 'My foot just slipped.'